ç

English for Academic Research

Series Editor
Adrian Wallwork, English for Academics SAS
Pisa, Italy

This series aims to help non-native, English-speaking researchers communicate in English. The books are designed like manuals or user guides to help readers find relevant information quickly, and assimilate it rapidly and effectively.

More information about this series at https://link.springer.com/bookseries/13913

Adrian Wallwork

Essential English Grammar and Communication Strategies

Intermediate Level

 Springer

Adrian Wallwork
English for Academics
Pisa, Italy

ISSN 2625-3445 ISSN 2625-3453 (electronic)
English for Academic Research
ISBN 978-3-030-95611-0 ISBN 978-3-030-95612-7 (eBook)
https://doi.org/10.1007/978-3-030-95612-7

This Springer imprint is published by the registered company Springer Nature Switzerland AG
The registered company address is: Gewerbestrasse 11, 6330 Cham, Switzerland

Introduction

Who is this book for? What are the aims of the book?

Who for: Non-native researchers, teachers of English for Academic Purposes (EAP).

Level of English: Intermediate and above.

Aims: A reference manual for learning the principal aspects of English that you need for academic writing.

- The grammar and link words needed to write a research paper.

- Strategies for ensuring what you write is easy for readers to understand.

- Strategies for writing clearly, unambiguously, with reasonably short sentences, and well-constructed paragraphs.

- Effective email communication with editors, referees and colleagues.

> This book thus includes only what is ESSENTIAL. It is NOT a comprehensive guide to grammar and usage.

If you want more detail then you can consult the following book, from which the present book has taken several examples:

English for Research: Usage, Style, and Grammar (SpringerNature).

This means that the present book <u>only</u> covers, for example, key areas of tense usage in academic writing (present simple, present perfect vs past simple, passive) and not less frequently used forms (e.g. conditionals). It focuses on those link words that create the least problems in terms of structure – thus words like *although*, *however* and *but* are covered, whereas *notwithstanding*, *nonetheless* and other less frequently used link words are not covered.

The idea was to create a book that:

- contains what you REALLY need to know

- provides simple strategies for carrying out quite complex tasks (e.g. difficult emails, reducing sentence length, writing unambiguously)

- you can study and learn from easily – the layout and examples are designed to be very clear. You can try to correct the bad examples by yourself, then check with the good examples

In some cases I have used examples that have appeared in my previous books. These books are mentioned at the end of the relevant section, so you can refer to them if you need more details.

Contents

Chapter 1
Articles and Nouns

1.1 a, an, one

a **before:**

- consonants
- the following letters in acronyms: B, C, D, G, J, K, P, Q, T, U, V, W, Y, Z
- *u*, if the sound is like <u>you</u> e.g. *university, unique, utility*
- *eu*
- *h* except in these cases: *an hour, an honor, an honest, an heir, an historical (a historical* is also common)

an **before:**

- *u*, if the *u* is pronounced as in *uncle, understanding, uninteresting*
- the following letters in acronyms: A, E, F, H, I, L, M, N, O, R, S, X

She has *a Apple* computer.

He has *an university* degree and *a* MBA.

She has *an Apple* computer.

He has *a university* degree and *an* MBA.

This is *a European* law.

This is *an EU* law.

This is *a universal* problem.

This is *an unusual* problem.

He is *an NBC* player.

A. Wallwork, *Essential English Grammar and Communication Strategies*,
English for Academic Research, https://doi.org/10.1007/978-3-030-95612-7_1

1.1   a, an, one (cont.)

one: indicates a number

I have written one paper not two.

There is only one way to do this.

Usage, Style, and Grammar: 3

Grammar Exercises: 3.2

All countable nouns (1.4) in the singular require an article (either *a/an* or *the*). You cannot say, for example, *I am without ticket*. But instead you should say *I don't have a ticket* or *the ticket*.

If a noun is uncountable, then *a/an* are not used. You cannot say *I need an information*, instead you can use *some* or *a piece of,* or in some cases simply omit the article.

We carried out the experiments *in laboratory*.

They work *in bank*.

This test gave *an information* about how to ...

They speak *a good English*.

Please give us *a feedback*.

1.1   a, an, one (cont.)

We carried out the experiments *in a / the laboratory*.

They work *in a bank*.

This test gave *some information* about how to ...

They speak *good English*.

Please give us *some feedback*.

Usage, Style, and Grammar: 3

Grammar Exercises: 3.1, 3.3

1.2   *a* vs *the*

a/an – generic, or first time you mention something

the - on subsequent occasions (i.e. when the reader already knows what you are talking about)

This paper presents *a* new system for modeling 4D maps. *The* system is based on ...

ABSTRACT In this work, we make *an* attempt to test the efficiency of ... CONCLUSIONS In this work, *the* attempt to assess the relative efficiency of the tested methods was carried out on two levels.

A comparison of our data with those in the literature indicates that ...

The comparison given in Sect. 2.1 highlights that ...

This is *a* first step = **an initial step** towards combatting the new virus. We cannot be sure of the outcome ...

This is *the* first step towards combatting the new virus. The second step is to ...

Usage, Style, and Grammar: 3

Grammar Exercises: 3.3

1.3   *the* vs no article

no article (also known as zero article) - to refer to something in general

the - to refer to something specific

the is not usually used with languages, but **the** is used with nationalities

Shortage of *water* in *Middle East* could be *cause* of *next world* war.

The researchers all over the world spend a lot of time in *laboratory*.

The drug is a serious problem in *the today's society*.

English made a terrible mistake to leave the European Union.

(Conclusions) *Results* show that x = y.

The shortage of *water* in *the* Middle East could be *the* cause of *the* next world war.

Our initial analysis proved that *the water* in the lake was very polluted.

Researchers all over the world spend a lot of time in *the* laboratory.

The researchers in our department spend a lot of time in *the* laboratory.

Drugs are a serious problem in today's society.

The English made a terrible mistake to leave the European Union.

English is a relatively easy language.

(Conclusions) *The / our* results show that x = y.

Pollution is a serious environmental issue and *the pollution* we have here in China is about the worst in the world.

Usage, Style, and Grammar: 3

Grammar Exercises: 3.4 – 3.9

1.4 Countable vs Uncountable Nouns

Countable - something that you can count and easily differentiate from other things of the same kind:

one car, two cars, three cars, many cars

Uncountable – difficult to count because not easy to divide up into distinct parts:

water, some water, a little water

I read *book*.

I read *two / many / various book*.

I received good *feedbacks*.

We need more *equipments*.

They have *few moneys*.

I have *an expertise* in this field.

I read *a / the / your* book.

I read two / many / various *books*.

I received good *feedback*.

We need more *equipment*.

They have *little money*.

I have [*some*] *expertise* in this field.

- When a countable noun is in the singular form, related words must be singular too.
- When a countable noun is plural, related words must be plural too.
- An uncountable noun is ALWAYS singular, so related words must be singular too.

1.4 Countable vs Uncountable Nouns (cont.)

This book are very interesting.

These informations are important. *They* must be read carefully.

These feedback is important.

We have done many *researches. These show* that x = y.

This book is very interesting.

This information is important. *It* must be read carefully.

This feedback is important.

We have done *a lot of research. This shows* that x = y.

Uncountable nouns used in academia: *access, accommodation, advertising, advice, agriculture* (and other subjects of study), *capital, cancer* (and other diseases and illnesses), *consent, electricity* (and other intangibles), *English* (and other languages), *equipment, evidence, expertise, feedback, functionality, gold* (and other metals), *hardware, health, industry, inflation, information, intelligence, knowhow, machinery, money, news, oxygen* (and other gases), *personnel, progress, research, safety, security, software, staff, storage, traffic, training, transport, waste, wealth, welfare, wildlife*

The table below lists words that indicate an indefinite quantity. These are words that you can generally use with countable and uncountable nouns in a research paper. Note: *a piece of* is not commonly used in research papers.

1.4 Countable vs Uncountable Nouns (cont.)

QUANTIFIER	COUNTABLE (SINGULAR)	COUNTABLE (PLURAL)	UNCOUNTABLE
a / an	a book		a piece of information
a (large / small) amount of		a large amount of books	a small amount of information
a bit / piece of			a piece of information
a few		a few books	
a great deal of		a great deal of books	a great deal of information
a little			a little information
a lot of		a lot of books	a lot of information
a number of		a number of books	
a series of		a series of books	
all		all the books	all the information
any		any books	any information
each	each book		each piece of information
enough		enough books	enough information
every	every book		every bit of information
few		few books	
little			little information
many		many books	many pieces of information
most		most books	most (of the) information
much			much (of the) information
no	no book	no books	no information
none of		none of the books	none of the information
one	one book		one piece of information
several		several books	
some		some books	some information
the	the book	the books	the information

Usage, Style, and Grammar: 1, 6.1

Grammar Exercises: 1

1.5   few, little, a few, a little; many, much

a little, a few = not much, not many

little, few = almost nothing / none; a very low (probably insufficient) quantity

a little, **little**, **much** + singular uncountable noun (1.4)

a few, **few**, **many** + plural noun

Few days ago we sent the paper to the editor.

We only had *little time* to undertake the research.

We have *few informations* on this topic.

A few days ago we sent the paper to the editor.

We only had *a little time* to undertake the research = A few days/weeks ...

We had *little time*. = A couple of days ...

We *don't have much information* on this topic.

= We only have *a little information*.

= We have *little information*.

Note the differences between these pairs of sentences.

He knows *a little* about this subject. = Just a few things.

He knows *little* about this subject. = He knows almost nothing.

Few people know this. = Hardly anyone / Almost no one knows about this.

A few people know this. = Some people know this, but not many.

Little has been done to help the poor. = Not enough / Very little has been done.

A little has been done to help the poor. = Something has been done, so a minimum amount of progress is being made.

1.5 few, little, a few, a little; many, much (cont.)

Usage, Style, and Grammar: 6.4

Vocabulary Exercises: 1.32

Grammar Exercises: 4.4, 4.5

Chapter 2
Abbreviations, Acronyms, False Friends, Spelling

2.1   Abbreviations (*Fig., App. ...*)

Only use abbreviations for words such as *figure* and *appendix*, when such words are associated with a number.

When you use an abbreviation: insert a period (.) after the abbreviation, insert a space before the number, and use a capital letter (*see Fig. 4*).

Don't begin a sentence with an abbreviation.

See also 5.4.

See the *fig.* below.

See the *Figure* below.

See *fig.* 5.

See *Fig.5*.

Fig. 5 shows that ...

See *the figure* below.

See *Figure* 5.

= See *Fig. 5.*

Figure 5 shows that ...

A. Wallwork, *Essential English Grammar and Communication Strategies*, English for Academic Research, https://doi.org/10.1007/978-3-030-95612-7_2

2.1 Abbreviations *(Fig., App. ...)* (cont.)

Usage, Style, and Grammar: 23

Grammar Exercises: 17.2

2.2 Acronyms

The first time you use an acronym, write the word out in full, followed by the acronym in brackets. Afterwards, just use the acronym.

Each letter of an acronym is usually capitalized.

Orders are dealt with on a *FIFO (first in first out)* basis.

We are part of a *Nasa* project.

Orders are dealt with on *a first in first out (FIFO)* basis.

We are part of a *NASA* project.

Don't use initial capital letters for the words that make up the acronym unless these words are generally found with capital letters in the literature (e.g. FAO, UNICEF, NATO).

The *Quality-of-Service* (QoS) requirements for …

Many *Small to Medium Enterprises* (SMEs) in Greece are family-owned.

The *world health organization* (WHO) was founded in 1948.

The *quality-of-service* (QoS) requirements for …

Many *small to medium enterprises* (SMEs) in Greece are family-owned.

The *World Health Organization* (WHO) was founded in 1948.

2.2 Acronyms (cont.)

Usage, Style, and Grammar: 22

100 Tips to Avoid Mistakes: 72

Grammar Exercises: 17.1

2.3   i.e., e.g., etc., et al.

The words below derive from Latin. Unless your journal states otherwise, they do NOT need to be in italics.

i.e. - defines

e.g. – gives examples

etc. = and so on

Note: the above can also be written *eg*, *ie*, *etc* (without the period [.])

et al. – and other authors, and colleagues. (*et al* is also used without a period)

et al.'s – genitive form of *et al.*

Great Britain, i.e. England, Scotland and Wales, is the ninth biggest island in the world and the third most populated. **(Great Britain is made up of only those three countries).**

Some EU members, e.g. Spain, Italy and France, are not in agreement with this policy. **(Spain, Italy and France are just some examples of countries in the European Union, there are also others).**

According to Smith et al. (2023), there are only three countries involved.

Smith et al.'s findings (2025) indicate that ...

Don't use e.g. at the beginning of a sentence.

Don't use e.g. when it does not introduce a list.

Sub-Saharan Africa, e.g., has a very high incidence, with 50% of raw cereal grains infected by the diseases.

This is true of many countries. E.g. the USA, the UK and Australia all ...

Sub-Saharan Africa, for example, has a very high incidence, with 50% of raw cereal grains infected by the diseases.

This is true of many countries. For example the USA, the UK and Australia all ...

2.3   i.e., e.g., etc., et al. (cont.)

Avoid redundancy:

Several countries, *such as, for example*, Gabon, Botswana and Angola, have introduced this policy.

Many countries have introduced this policy, *e.g.* Eritrea, Guinea-Bissau, Djibouti, South Sudan *etc*.

Several countries, *such as* Gabon, Botswana and Angola, have introduced this policy.

Many countries have introduced this policy*, e.g.* Eritrea, Guinea-Bissau, Djibouti, and South Sudan.

Usage, Style, and Grammar: 13.10, 13.11

100 Tips to Avoid Mistakes: 45

Vocabulary Exercises:2.18, 2.19

Writing Exercises: 4.7

2.4 False Friends

A **false friend** is a word in your language that looks the same as word in English, but has a different meaning. One that frequently appears in research is to *control* (= to regulate), whose false friend in many other languages means to *verify*. Here is the difference:

A thermostat is used to *control* the temperature.

We *checked* the patient's temperature with a thermometer.

Below are 20 false friends that may cause problems in scientific papers.

	MEANS	DOES NOT MEAN
accurate	correct in all details	comprehensive, thorough
actually	really, in reality	currently, at the moment
argument	heated discussion	subject, topic
assist	help	attend, participate, be present
biological	relating to organisms	organic, environmentally-friendly
coherent	logical and consistent, understandable	consistent
consistent	always done in same way	coherent
control	exert power, regulate	check, verify
convenient	suitable, situated nearby	inexpensive
economical	not expensive to run	inexpensive
education	what you learn at school	upbringing (what you learn at home)
eventually	in the end (after some trouble)	if necessary, in the likely course of events
fabric	material, cloth	factory
proper	correct, suitable, right	own, customized
realize	begin to understand	create, develop
sensible	reasonable, practical	sensitive
suggestive	making one think of, allusive	evocative, with interesting possibilities
territory	land under national jurisdiction	local area
unique	the only one of its kind	single, individual, one
valorize	give validity, raise value artificially	upcycle, enhance, improve, exploit

Vocabulary Exercises: 6.1, 6.2

2.5 Spelling

Poor spelling in Anglo countries is often associated with a lack of education. It is also a sign that the author did not carry out her / his work very accurately and is thus not a reliable researcher.

Before you send anyone an important document, the last check you should do is the spelling check. If you are using Microsoft Word, ensure that you follow this procedure:

1. select US or UK spelling according to the journal's requirements (*Tools – Language*)
2. check that under *Language* you have NOT ticked *Do not check spelling or grammar*
3. under *Tools – Spelling and Grammar* select *Reset Ignored Words and Grammar*. This feature enables you to make the entire document uniform in terms of spelling (your doc may be made up of several cuts and pastes from other docs which may have different spellings set)
4. select Editor – this enables you to check both the spelling and the grammar. The grammar suggestions are often very useful (repeated words, punctuation, more concise ways of saying the same thing)

Use the most recent version of your spelling / grammar program.

Remember that the spelling software will not find all the typos (spelling errors) in your doc, particularly the ones listed in the table below (which are just a few of the many possible errors).

Misspellings that spell-checking software does not necessarily find

Some misspellings will not be highlighted because they are words that really exist. Note that these are just examples, there are many other possible mistakes of this type.

2.5 Spelling (cont.)

WORD	EXAMPLE	WORD	EXAMPLE
addition (n)	The addition of gold led to higher values.	addiction (n)	Their addiction to cannabis had led to behavioral problems.
analyzes/ses (v)	The software analyzes the data.	analyses (n pl., sing. analysis)	We carried out two analyses.
assess (v)	We assess the pros and cons.	asses (n pl)	Horses and asses (*equus asinus*).
attached (p.p.)	Please find attached our manuscript.	attacked (p.p.)	Violent mobs attacked the Capitol.
context (n)	The meaning of a word may depend on the context.	contest (n)	This is basically a contest in which no one wins.
chose (inf. choose)	In the past we always chose this method because ...	choice (n)	The rationale behind our choice was ...
drawn (inf. draw)	Conclusions are drawn in Sect. 5	drown (inf)	They drowned because they could not swim.
fell (inf. fall)	The tree fell on the house.	felt (inf. feel)	The patients said they all felt anxious.
filed (inf. file)	It is filed under 'docs'.	field (n)	The field of ICT is ever growing.
form (v)	We would like to form a new group.	from (prep)	Professor Yang comes from China.
found (inf. find)	We found very high values in ...	founded (inf. found)	IBM was founded in 1911.
lose (inf.)	Companies may lose a lot of money.	loose (adj)	There is only a loose connection between the two.
rely (v)	We rely on CEOs to make good decisions.	relay (v, n)	This relays the information to the train's onboard computer.
than (conj, adv)	This is better than that.	then (adv)	After Stage 1, we then added the liquid.
thanks (n pl)	Thanks are due to the following people:	tanks (n)	The fish were stored in water tanks.
though (adv, conj)	The overheads are high, though the performance is excellent.	tough (adj)	This is a tough question to answer.
through (prep)	This was achieved through a comparative study of ...	trough (n)	Pigs eat from a trough.
two	Two replications were made.	tow (v)	The car is equipped to tow a caravan.
three (n)	Tests were repeated three times.	tree	Tests were conducted on an apple tree.
underlying (adj)	The main points underlying the application of this procedure are ...	underling (n)	An underling is a person of lower status or rank.
use (v, n)	We use a method developed by ...	sue (v)	Patients frequently sue their physicians for malpractice.

2.5 Spelling (cont.)

WORD	EXAMPLE	WORD	EXAMPLE
weighed (inf. weigh)	The samples were dried and then weighed.	weighted (adj)	The weighted values were obtained by dividing the integral of the ...
which (pronoun)	This worked well, which was surprising considering that ...	witch (n)	Life often ended early for a witch in medieval times – burnt on the stake.
with (conj)	We worked with them in 2023.	whit (n)	Whit is a religious festival.

US vs UK (British) spelling

Check which spelling system your journal requires. This information should be contained in the journal's "Instructions to Authors". Below are just a few examples of differences between the two spelling systems.

UK in blue, US in black.

   aluminium, aluminum; anaemia, anemia; anaesthesia, anesthesia; analogue, analog; analyse, analyze; archaeology, archeology; artefact, artifact; backwards, backward; behaviour, behavior; catalogue, catalog; centre, center; colour, color; defence, defense; dialogue, dialog; empower, impower/empower; ensure, insure/ensure; fibre, fiber; flavour, flavor; forwards, forward; grey, gray; labelled, labeled; licence (n), license (n, v); license (v), license (n, v); materialise, materialize; metre, meter; modelled, modeled; modeller, modeler; oedema, edema; offence, offense; practice (n), practise (n, v); programme, program; realise, realize; sulphur, sulfur; towards, toward; travelled, traveled; traveller, traveler

Both *-ize* and *-ise* are common in UK spelling.

Let's hope that one day the scientific world will see sense and just adopt one system – preferably the US system as it is more simple and more logical!

2.5   Spelling (cont.)

Usage, Style, and Grammar: 28

100 Tips to Avoid Mistakes: 73

Vocabulary Exercises: 7.1, 7.2

Writing Exercises: 1.11

Chapter 3
Can, May, Could, Might

can, may, could and *might* are known as 'modal verbs'. The exact rules for these words are complex and subtle. This chapter outlines only how these words are typically used when writing papers or giving presentations, so not in spoken English or informal written English. However, some examples are given from general English when this helps to make the differences between two modal verbs easier to understand.

The first section begins with the difference between *cannot* and *may not*. In fact, if you can understand the difference between these two negative forms, this will help you understand how they are used in the affirmative form (*can* vs *may*).

There are other modal verbs (*must, need, should* etc), however these do not normally lead to ambiguity and are much easier to use. For details on how to use them see Chapter 12 in *Usage, Style, and Grammar* in the *English for Academic Research* series.

© The Author(s), under exclusive license to Springer Nature
Switzerland AG 2022
A. Wallwork, *Essential English Grammar and Communication Strategies*,
English for Academic Research, https://doi.org/10.1007/978-3-030-95612-7_3

3.1   impossibility and possibility: *cannot* vs *may not*

cannot - something that is <u>not</u> possible

may not – a <u>possibility</u> that something will not happen, or a certain event or scenario is not likely

I **cannot** come to the lesson tomorrow because I am on holiday. = It is impossible for me to come.

I **may not** come to the lesson – I will let you know later today if I can or not. = Perhaps I will not come.

She **cannot** be at home yet; she doesn't stop work until after 6 pm.

I would try ringing her later because she **may not** be at home yet.

I'm afraid our results are not ready, so we **cannot** submit our paper yet.

I am not sure if our results will be ready on time, so we **may not** be able to meet the deadline for submission.

Although x showed similarities to y, we **cannot** rule out that such similarities are only coincidental.

These differences **may not** be due to the intrinsic properties of the materials, but could be the result of the sampling method.

Shakespeare was not born until 1564. So this work (dated 1560) **cannot** have been written by him.

Although our sample was only small, this **may not** have affected the results because the sample was, in any case, very representative.

3.2 present and future ability and possibility: *can* vs *may*

can - a characteristic behavior. When certain conditions are met or desired, *can* indicates that things are possible but do not necessarily happen. *can* is also often another way of saying *I am able to*

may - a potential for something to happen. It indicates uncertainty and is thus used to make hypotheses, to speculate about the future, or to talk about probability

I **can** send you the document tomorrow. = *I am certain that I will be able to send document tomorrow.*

I **may** come to the meeting. = *Perhaps I will come.*

I **can** come next Wednesday at 12 o'clock - so note that down in your diary.

He **may** come next week, but he's not sure at the moment.

Sometimes there is really no difference in meaning.

Using the wrong method **can / may** affect the results, but not necessarily.

Sometimes the values **can / may** be as high as 10.

When you talk about a future possibility, use *may* and not *can.*

In this particular case, there is a risk that dust **may** become attached to the surface. = This is a probability but not a certainty.

Because dust **can** become attached to the surface, the tests need to be carried out in the clean room. = This is a regular event (i.e. it doesn't refer to one specific case but can be extended to all similar cases).

Sometimes phrases containing *can* are redundant or can be made more concise.

This **can** be considered useful in cases where ... = This is useful in cases where ...

The properties **can** vary considerably. = The properties vary considerably.

Defects **can** be identified on the surfaces. = There are defects on the surfaces.

As **can** be seen in Figure 3, the values of x are ... Figure 3 shows that the values ...

Typical uses of *can + be +* past participle:

More details **can** be found in Section 1.

This difference **can** be explained / calculated / measured by taking into account that ...

In this case, friction **can** be expressed as: $\mu \approx \tau_m \bullet A_n / F_N$

3.3 *could* – use for hypothetical situations rather than to express ability

could – in papers, tends only to be used to make a <u>hypothesis</u>. In the first example below, *could* basically means the same as *may*. In the second case, only *could* is appropriate.

This discrepancy **could / may** be due to the different sampling methods used.

Given these limitations, a future research avenue **could** be to use a much larger sample.

Do NOT use **could** (in the affirmative) to refer to something that you were able to do (i.e. that you were successful in doing) in the lab. Instead use one of the alternative forms given below.

Despite the level of complexity, we **could** calculate the values.

Despite the level of complexity, we **calculated** the values.

... we **managed to calculate** the values.

... we **were able to calculate** the values.

... we **succeeded in calculating** the values.

Avoid *could be* + past participle when you could simply replace it with *was/were*.

In any case, no discrepancies **could be** found. = We looked for discrepancies but were unable to find them.

In any case, no discrepancies **were** found. = We were not actively looking for them and in any case none came to light.

Based on the literature [25], these values **could be** consigned to the first category. = in the future

Based on the literature [25], these values **were** consigned to the first category. = in the past

3.3   *could* – use for hypothetical situations rather than to express ability (cont.)

could not (i.e. the negative) <u>is</u> grammatically correct to refer to something that you were NOT able to do, but again it tends to be replaced by an alternative form.

Given the level of complexity, we **could** not calculate the values. *

... we **were unable to calculate** ...

... we **did not manage to calculate** ...

... we **did not succeed in calculating** ...

* *we could not calculate the values* is ambiguous. It is not clear, whether in situations of complexity nobody even attempts to make this calculation, or whether in this particular case an attempt was made to do the calculation but the level of complexity was so high that the attempt failed. All the phrases in blue refer to either a successful attempt (e.g. *we were able*) or a failed attempt (e.g. *we were not able*).

3.4   deductions and speculations: *can* and *could vs might*

Unfortunately, there are no clear rules for when you should use *might instead of could, can or may*. So rather than rules, this section just gives examples with explanations.

Future research **could** be directed towards elucidating this pathology.

(A suggestion on one of the possible areas for future research).

Such research **might** then reveal the true causes of this pathology.

(This is just a hypothesis; we cannot be sure that the research will reveal the cause. *may* could be used here but it would, perhaps, indicate greater certainty).

One solution **could** be to get parents and children to swap roles for a day.

(A suggestion, proposal – something that is feasible)

What if parents and children swapped roles for a day? How **might** they behave differently?

(A hypothetical question for which there is no certain answer. *would* could also be used here with little difference in meaning).

This **cannot** be the reason why the first two experiments gave very different results. There must be another reason ...

(An impossibility = 100% certainty)

This **might (may) not** be the only reason why the first two experiments gave very different results. It is likely that there are other explanations ...

(This is a possibility, but we are not certain that it is true)

Chapter 4
Clarity and Empathy

4.1   Clear and Concise Writing vs Redundancy

Avoid writing in a complicated way or filling your sentences with elegant-sounding redundancy. Instead, write clearly and concisely.

The sentences below all contain redundancy.

1. It was yellow in colour and round in shape.
2. This will be done in the month of December.
3. During the maturation process, the plant grows to ten times its original size.
4. We did x. This choice meant that ...
5. As can be seen, Figure 1 shows that x = y.
6. The activity aimed at the extrapolation of X is not trivial.
7. The summary statements presented above represent the authors' current perceptions in relation to the results. Since the work is ongoing, these statements should only be viewed as conclusions to the extent that it is the author's intention and aim to embellish them in the light of subsequent events.

The words that could be removed are in italics below. In the case of the last example, the two sentences have been removed entirely. By removing unnecessary words you will probably also remove some mistakes.

It was yellow *in colour* and round *in shape*. You may not be sure if you require the word *shape* or another word, for example, *form*. If you delete it, you avoid making a mistake.

This will be done in *the month of* December. *month* is generic, *December* is specific. If possible, just use the specific word.

4.1   Clear and Concise Writing vs Redundancy (cont.)

During the maturation *process*, the plant grows to ten times its original size. Maturation is a process - avoid pointless abstract words.

We did x. This *choice* meant that … You may get confused with the spelling (*choice, choose, chose*).

As can be seen, Figure 1 highlights that x = y. Cut redundant phrases at the beginning of a sentence. Try to put the subject at the beginning instead.

The *activity aimed at the* extrapolation of X is not trivial. You may not know if it is *aim at* or *aim to*. Passive: *This is aimed at + ing.* Active: *We aim to + infinitive.*

The summary statements presented above represent the authors' current perceptions in relation to the results. Since the work is ongoing, these statements should only be viewed as conclusions to the extent that it is the author's intention and aim to embellish them in the light of subsequent events. If you are particularly pleased with something you have written, because it sounds very eloquent or shows the high level of your English, then DELETE IT!

If you cut redundant words it is impossible to make mistakes with them! They add no value for the reader. They are not concrete.

4.2 Reduce the number of NON key words so that the real key words stand out

The key words in the two examples below are the same.

But in the red example there are 58 non-key words, i.e. generic words with no real value for the reader. In the blue example there are only 26 non-key words.

If you reduce the non-key words, your key words will stand out more from the text and will be noticed more by the reader.

Even though **GC/MS and GC-C-IRMS** are the main techniques reported in the literature for the study of **organic residues**, recently, we have seen an increasing in the application of **high-resolution mass spectrometry (HRMS)** mainly coupled with liquid chromatography. It provides the opportunity for performing **accurate mass measurements**, and has shown its enormous capability to **distinguish isobaric compounds** thanks to the determination of **exact molecular mass and elemental composition**. In addition, when the instrumental asset makes it possible, the **interpretation of tandem mass spectra** allows the elucidation of **chemical structures**, even in the case of **isomers**, to be obtained.

GC/MS and GC-C-IRMS are the key techniques for studying **organic residues**. However, **high-resolution mass spectrometry (HRMS)** coupled with **liquid chromatography** is becoming more common. Through **accurate mass measurements, HRMS** differentiates between **isobaric compounds** by determining the **exact molecular mass and elemental composition**. In addition, **tandem mass spectra** can potentially reveal the underlying **chemical structures**, even for **isomers**.

If you reduce the number of non-key words:

- Quicker for reader to read.

- Your key words and your key points will stand out much more.

- You will be cited more in other papers, because your paper will be more readable and thus your key findings will be easier to see (i.e. not hidden by extraneous words) and to understand.

4.3   Use more verbs and fewer nouns

Prefer verbs to nouns.

Prefer a verb to a <u>verb + noun</u> construction.

X was used in the calculation of Y.

This allows the analysis of X to be performed.

A comparison was made between X and Y.

X showed a better performance than Y.

X was used *to calculate* Y.

This allows you to *analyse* X.

= This allows X to *be analysed.*

X and Y were *compared.*

X *performed* better than Y.

You can write more succinctly and still:

1. retain the same information

2. be 100% clear

English for Writing Research Papers (2016 edn.): Chapters 5, 6, 7, 8

100 Tips to Avoid Mistakes: Chapters 5 and 6

4.4 Always think about the point of view of your readers / audience. By helping them you are also helping yourself

Do NOT focus on making the writing process easy for you. Instead, focus on making the reading process easy for your readers, or the listening process easy for the audience at a conference.

- Write and speak clearly – <u>generally</u> with short sentences
- Choose a layout that is easy to see, read and understand
- Give concrete concepts with lots of clear examples
- Use the minimum number of words, pages, slides, info

By helping the

1. readers of your paper
2. recipients of your emails
3. audience of your presentation

you are also helping yourself. If they understand what you have written or said, they will

1. continue reading and hopefully cite you in their papers
2. reply quickly to your emails
3. contact you after the presentation

Think in terms of ***them them them*** NOT *me me me*. What do **they** want to know? Read first? Hear first? How can I make it easier for **them**?

Your papers need to be written in good clear English, so that:

- editors and reviewers will understand the novelty of your research and your key findings
- readers will find it easy to understand and remember, and be encouraged to cite your paper in their paper. The more cites you get, the higher you rise in the publishing hierarchy.

4.5 Present information in the simplest and most logical way possible

The red example requires minimal effort by you the **writer**, but maximum effort for your **readers**.

The blue example requires minimal effort for the READER. But it requires more effort for you the writer because it means you have to organize your thoughts very clearly.

Human memory can be subdivided into **sensory memory** (by which we see a film as a continuous scene rather than a series of still images), **short-term memory** (as used for example when you mentally calculate 3 × 7 × 4), **declarative-learning long-term memory** (i.e. conscious recollection, for example of last week's English class), and **procedural-learning long-term memory** (of *how* to do something, for example play the piano).

There are **four main types** of human memory. **First**, sensory memory, for example we see a film as a continuous scene rather than a series of still images. **Second**, short-term memory, this helps for example when you mentally calculate 3 × 7 × 4. **Third**, we have declarative-learning long-term memory. This means conscious recollection, for example, of last week's English class. **Finally**, procedural-learning long-term memory reminds us *how* to do something, for example play the piano.

The more difficult a task is, the more negative the emotions attached to it, and the more difficult it is for …

- the reader to find your key results in a paper
- your audience to understand a graph in your presentation
- your recipient to find/understand your request in an email
- a Human Resources manager to find info on your CV

4.5 Present information in the simplest and most logical way possible (cont.)

The point is **not** complexity and 'elegance'. The point is **not** good vs bad.

The point is: is this text **effective** or not?

If you want:

- referees to accept your paper
- readers to understand you
- your research proposals to be funded
- your CV to be read and understood (so that you get a job)
- people to reply to your emails

Use short simple sentences (but see 9.3) and short paragraphs in everything you write (papers, slides, emails, CVs, tweets).

> There is a direct correlation between "poor English" and lower chances of publication, and fewer chances that your emails, CVs, proposals etc will be read and responded to.

Reviewers and readers do NOT want:

- Unnecessary effort (long sentences, poor organization, <u>redundancy</u>)
- Findings that are not highlighted
- Ambiguity / Unclear sentences
- Contribution / Innovation not clear
- Spelling mistakes

All the above show lack of empathy for the reader. The reader is forced to try to make sense of poorly written work. Papers and projects are NOT normally rejected for a few grammar or vocabulary mistakes. But CVs are rejected even for just one mistake.

Projects and papers ARE rejected because they require too much mental effort by the reviewers.

4.5 Present information in the simplest and most logical way possible (cont.)

English for Writing Research Papers (2016 edn.): 1.9, 1.12, 1.13, 2.3; and Chapters 3, 5, 6, and 20

100 Tips: Chapters 5 and 7

4.6   Avoid ambiguity with pronouns

Some sentences that would not be ambiguous in your language (because you have masculine and feminine nouns) may become ambiguous in English. For example:

I put the book in the car and then I left it there all day.

In English we do not know whether *it* refers to the book or the car.

I put the *book* in the car and then I left the *book* there all day.

You may think that repeating the key word is not very elegant, but it is much clearer for your reader and is not considered bad style in technical English.

If you use pronouns and expressions such as *it, them, this, that, one, the other, the former, the latter* to refer to a noun you have mentioned in a previous sentence, you may be forcing to the reader to re-read the previous sentence to remember what the pronoun refers to. So if you think that there could be possible ambiguity or that the reader may have forgotten the subject, then simply repeat the key word.

We could go to Australia, Canada or the Netherlands, but *they* are a long way from here. [Does *they* refer to all three locations, to Canada and the Netherlands, or just to the Netherlands?]

No usernames or passwords are required, unless the system administrator decides that *one* is necessary. … decides that *this* is necessary. … decides that *these* are necessary. [What do *one / this / these* refer to? a) usernames b) passwords?]

We cut the trees into sectors, then separated the logs from the branches, and then burnt *them*. [Does *them* refer to just the *branches* or the *logs* as well?

To avoid misunderstandings, be more specific:

Australia, Canada or the Netherlands, *all of which* are a long way from here.

Australia, Canada or the Netherlands. But *Canada and the Netherlands* are a long way from here.

4.6   Avoid ambiguity with pronouns (cont.)

Australia, Canada or the Netherlands. But *the Netherlands* are a long way from here.

... unless the system administrator decides that a *username* is necessary.

... unless the system administrator decides that a *password* is necessary.

We cut the trees into sectors, then separated the logs from the branches, and then burnt the *branches*.

See also the former / the latter (8.6).

he / she / they

Never use **he** to refer to a generic person. If possible use **they**, even if the subject is singular. Note that some people may find **he/she** offensive, so again use **they**. The same guidelines apply to *his, her, hers, their, theirs*.

If you go to the doctor and *he* tells you that ...
The user can decide whether *he/she* needs to change the password or not.

If you go to the doctor and *they* tell you that ...

The user can decide whether *they* need to change the password or not.

Users can decide whether *they* need to change the password or not.

4.7 Ensure that there is no ambiguity when you use the passive

Be very careful of the passive when comparing your work with previous work in the literature.

Some journals in their Instructions to Authors prohibit the use of personal pronouns (*we*). Such journals are misguided to make this prohibition as it often leads to ambiguity. In fact, the passive form does not tell the reader with 100% certainty who performed the action.

When you are talking about the literature (typically in the Introduction and Discussion) and you use the passive to refer <u>both</u> to your own work <u>and</u> to the literature, the reader will have difficulty understanding if YOU did something or an ANOTHER AUTHOR did it. Instead, when referring to YOUR work use *we* and *our study / work / research*.

In the example below, it is impossible to understand who has made or is making the assumption.

Children are conditioned by their parents [1, 7, 9]. Thus it is assumed that children in orphanages will behave differently. In fact ...

Children are conditioned by their parents [1, 7, 9]. Thus it is generally assumed that children in orphanages will behave differently [12, 17]. In fact,

Children are conditioned by their parents [1, 7, 9]. It is well known that children who have been abandoned by their parents will ...

Note how *generally* and *it is well known* indicate that these are <u>not</u> just the author's viewpoints. Also the references to the literature ([12,17]) help the reader to understand that this information has already been published and is thus in the public domain.

4.8 Be careful when using expressions such as *in a previous work*

It must be very clear that you are talking about YOUR own previous work, rather than the previous work of an author you have just mentioned.

In the examples below Ying is another author. Alvarez is the author of the present paper,

Ying et al noted that red is most people's favorite color. However, *in a previous work* [24], *it was noted* that green was ...

Ying et al noted that red is most people's favorite color. However, in a previous work *carried out by our group* [Alvarez, 2021], *we noted* that green was ...

In the blue example above, everything is clear for the reader. This is because the author has written two key phrases: carried out by <u>our</u> group ... <u>we</u> noted that ...

Summary: Use *we* and *our* to differentiate between your work and the work of others. If you don't, you will create confusion for the reader. This is one of the biggest mistakes made in academic writing.

100 Tips to Avoid Mistakes: 39

Chapter 5
Comparisons, Dates, Measurements, Numbers

5.1 Comparisons

Most multi-syllable adjectives form their comparison and superlative with *more* and *most*. Examples:

more intelligent, the most useful, more polite, the most common

All adjectives of one syllable, and adjectives that end in *–y* or *–ow*, add *-er* or *-ier*. Examples:

easy > easier, easiest; happy > happier, happiest; narrow > narrower, narrowest

Irregular adjectives:

good, better, the best; bad, worse, the worst; little, less, the least; much, more, the most; far, further / farther; the furthest / farthest

To compare two people, things or events, use a comparative adjective + *than*, or a noun + *than*:

A Ferrari is more expensive than a Fiat.

There is more information than I was expecting.

To show that there is no difference between people, things or events, use *as* + adjective/noun + *as*. If there is a difference use *as* + adjective/noun + *as*:

Britain's GDP is as big as Italy's GDP.

I am *worst* than you at English.

It was the *more expensive* I could find.

She is *the better* in the class.

The new reservoir holds ten times water *as much as* the old one.

This exercise is *more easy* than that one.

A. Wallwork, *Essential English Grammar and Communication Strategies*, English for Academic Research, https://doi.org/10.1007/978-3-030-95612-7_5

5.1 Comparisons (cont.)

I am *worse* than you at English.

It was the *most expensive* I could find.

She is *the best* in the class.

The new reservoir holds ten times *as much water as* the old one.

This exercise is *easier* than that one.

Usage, Style, and Grammar: 19

Grammar Exercises: 15

5.2   Dates

Day + month: there is no need to use ˢᵗ, ᵗʰ, and ʳᵈ. Simply write the day as follows: 10 March.

Full dates: 10 March 2030 = 10.03.2030 in Europe (and much of the world) = 03.10.2030 in the USA

Centuries: 19ᵗʰ century, 21ˢᵗ century (do not use Roman numerals)

Decades: 1960s, 2030s

Years: 257 BCE (before common era) and CE (common era) or 257 BPE (before present era) and PE (present era). BC (before Christ) and AD (anno domini) are also used but are becoming obsolete.

They can be dated to a time-span ranging from the *VII century* BCE to the *II century* CE.

This paper presents an analysis of the music of the *'90s / 1990's*.

They calculate that the world will end on 03.10.2060.

They can be dated to a time-span ranging from the *7th* century BCE to the *2nd* century CE.

This paper presents an analysis of the techno-rhythms of the music of the *1990s*.

Smith et al. calculate that the world will end on *10 March 2060* [3 October 2060 (US)]

Usage, Style, and Grammar: 21.12

5.3 Digits vs words (e.g. 8 vs *eight*)

In the main text (i.e. not in tables and figures) use digits for numbers above nine (i.e. 10, 11, 12, 355, 8760). Ignore this rule if there is a series of numbers that includes some numbers higher than nine. Generally speaking, use common sense – whatever you think is the clearest way for readers to immediately see and understand the number.

For the color measurements, *4* fruits of each cultivar were analyzed.

In the last *3* years the numbers have risen by 11, 6 and 7, respectively.

For the color measurements, *four* fruits of each cultivar were analyzed.

In the last *three* years the numbers have risen by 11, 6 and 7, respectively.

Do not mix words and digits to refer to the same number, unless this number is a million or more.

Avoid very long numbers with lots of zeros, try to use a shorter form instead.

Do not mix words and digits within the same context.

There were 200 thousand people at the conference.

More than half of the Earth's 7,800,000,000 inhabitants live in the tropics and subtropics.

There was a two- to 3-fold increase.

There were 200,000 people at the conference.

= There were two hundred thousand people at the conference.

More than half of the Earth's 7.8 billion inhabitants live in the tropics and subtropics.

There was a two- to three-fold increase.

5.4   Numbers in measurements and associated with table and figures

table and **figure**, when associated with a number, require an initial capital T and F. There is no abbreviation for table. The abbreviation for *figure* is *Fig.* – with a period after the *g*.

Abbreviations for quantities normally have a space before them, except in the case of percentages. However, usage various from journal to journal.

As shown in *table 3*, the patient was only tall *1.2m* and weighed *9kg*. Her percentage body fat was *9.9 %* (see *fig. 3* for details).

As shown in *Table 3*, the patient was only *1.20 m* tall and weighed *9 kg*. Her percentage body fat was *9.9%* (see *Fig. 3* for details).

5.5 Numbers at the beginning of a sentence

Do not use a digit at the beginning of a sentence. Instead use the word form (e.g. *Fifty* rather than *50*) or rearrange the sentence.

50% of users do not use this feature.

1.85 ml of distilled water was added to the mixture.

11 plants were infected.

Fifty percent of users do not use this feature.

= This feature is not used by *50%* of users.

An amount of 1.85 ml of distilled water was added to the mixture.

Eleven plants were infected. = *A total of 11* plants were infected.

Note how in the last sentence above the verb (*were infected*) is plural. The verb agrees with *plants* and not with *total*. Similarly in phrases that begin with *a series of, a quantity of*, the verb agrees with the noun that comes after *of*. However, some authors prefer the verb in the singular.

A series of experiments were/was conducted.

5.6   Differences between written and spoken forms of numbers

The table below explains how numbers are usually written (in a document) and said (for example in an oral presentation). Note that tens of numbers can be written *thirty seven* or *thirty-seven*: Microsoft Word suggests using the hyphen.

WRITTEN	SAID	WRITTEN	SAID
cardinals and ordinals			
101 213 1,123	a/one hundred and one two hundred and thirteen one thousand, one hundred and twenty three	58,679 2,130,362	fifty eight thousand six hundred and seventy nine two million, one hundred and thirty thousand, three hundred and sixty two
13th	thirteenth	31st	thirty first
calendar dates			
10.03.20 GB: day/month/ year US: month/day/ year	the tenth of March two thousand and twenty (GB) or March (the) tenth two thousand and twenty (GB) October third two thousand twenty (US)	2030 1996 1701	two thousand and thirty twenty thirty nineteen ninety six nineteen hundred and ninety six seventeen oh one seventeen hundred and one.
fractions, decimals, percentages			
¼	a quarter / one quarter	0.25	(zero) point two five
½	a half / one half	0.056	(zero) point zero five six
¾	three quarters	37.9	thirty seven point nine
10%	ten per cent	100%	one hundred percent
squares, cubes etc			
$4m^2$ $5m^3$	four meters squared, four square meters five cubic meters, five meters cubed	2^5	two to the power of five
money			
€678	six hundred and seventy eight euros	$450,617	four hundred fifty thousand six hundred seventeen dollars
¥1.50	one yen fifty (cents)	$1.90	a dollar ninety
measurements			
1m 70	one meter seventy	3.5kg	three point five kilos
3m x 6m	three meters by six		
100^0	one hundred degrees	-10^0	minus ten degrees ten degrees below zero

5.6 Differences between written and spoken forms of numbers (cont.)

Usage, Style, and Grammar: 21

Grammar Exercises: 16

5.7 Additional guidelines

When *hundred*, *thousand*, *billion* are preceded by another number (e.g. *three hundred*) no -s plural is required. You can only say *hundreds*, *thousands* etc to mean 'several hundred / thousand' (e.g. Hundreds / thousands of people are becoming victims every day).

When referring to measurements note the word order: I am two meters tall (verb + measurement + adjective).

The definite article (*the*) is NOT required before percentages (the 10%) and NOT before the numbers of questions in a list (Let us know turn to the item 3).

Chapter 6
CVS / Resumes

6.1   General guidelines

Your CV is one of the most important documents you will ever write. It is the one that gets you a job.

You are probably unable to judge your own level of English. So, show your CV to a qualified native English speaker and ask them to correct it for you. Even if you have to spend some money, this money will be well spent.

BUT avoid online services or automatic CV creators / templates. Instead contact someone you know and trust to draft or revise your CV.

Here are ten key guidelines.

1. Use a standard template e.g. Europass if you are in Europe. If not, look at documents produced by the institute/company where you want to work – use their font and style of layout.

2. Be honest.

3. Be concise, short and clear. No redundancy.

4. Put most important (and most recent) information first.

5. Be relevant: tell readers only what THEY need to know, not everything that YOU know

6. Be specific, not generic.

7. Find things that differentiate you from other possible candidates. Think about what makes you unique: sell yourself.

8. To save space use links to your department's homepage, your ResearchGate profile etc. But only 3-4 links max in the whole CV.

9. The amount of space (i.e. number of words and lines) that you dedicate to a particular section or subsection is generally an indicator of the importance of the information contained in that section. So the more important something is in terms of you getting a specific job, the more space you should dedicate to it, and vice versa.

10. Check your spelling. One spelling mistake may be enough for the reader (e.g. a human resources manager) to conclude that because you didn't check the spelling of your CV, you are an unreliable person.

© The Author(s), under exclusive license to Springer Nature   51
Switzerland AG 2022
A. Wallwork, *Essential English Grammar and Communication Strategies*,
English for Academic Research, https://doi.org/10.1007/978-3-030-95612-7_6

6.2 Sections

The following sections are generally (but not always) part of a CV.

1. Photo (consider not having a photo to show support for those who are discriminated against)

2. Personal data (6.3)

3. Executive summary (6.4)

4. Work experience (6.6)

5. Academic experience (6.6)

6. Skills (6.7, 6.8, 6.9)

7. Personal interests (6.10)

8. Projects, publications, conferences - possibly on a separate page, particularly if there are many of them

9. References (6.11)

6.3   Personal data

Name: no (this should be at top of CV)

Date and place of birth: yes (but not by law)

Nationality: yes (this may be needed to indicate that a visa is necessary)

Sex: No legal obligation to put this. You may consider putting it if you have no photo and your name gives no indication of your gender.

Marital status: not necessary

Contact details: just your email and your cell phone number

FB, Twitter, Instagram: No! But links to LinkedIn and ResearchGate are fine.

Avoid using icons. They take up space and are usually redundant.

To save space, write the information horizontally (rather than vertically) and centered.

Rajiv Khan

10 March 2003, Indian, + 91 340 7888 304, rajiv.khan@institute.edu

6.4   Executive Summary

An executive summary is like a mini abstract that describes your experience, qualifications and skills. It immediately gives the reader a very rapid overview of who you are. It is located under your Personal Details.

- 3-4 points (max 3 lines each), concise, no personal pronouns

- Full of key words (from the advert for the position or a similar position)

- Highlight the things that make you different from other candidates i.e. that make you uniquely qualified for the job

- Very specific: No generic unsubstantiated statements

Put your Executive Summary directly under your Personal Details. Below are two possible structures.

STRUCTURE 1 (HEADINGS)

Position desired: Research post in polymerization

Experience in syntheses of organic molecules and polymers especially fluorine-containing (meth)acrylate monomers, macromolecular initiators and macromolecules with controlled architecture.

Good knowledge of controlled radical polymerization methods e.g. ATRP, RAFT.

Future interests: Supramolecular polymers, controlled polymerization, hybrid organic-inorganic nanocomposites ...

STRUCTURE 2 (BULLET POINTS)

- Two years of development experience. Strong core Java/J2SE - especially in high performance multi-threaded server development.

- Three years of work experience at ABC Engineering (Tirana, Albania).

- Excellent knowledge of FIX and messaging based connectivity applications.

- Currently in final year of PhD in Virtual Robotics at the University of Tirana.

6.5 Dates

Date of birth: 5 November 2007

Institute / Workplace: 2023 – 2024; Dec 2029 - Jan 2030 (months are abbreviated to their first three letters. Only put months to indicate short periods of time)

6.6 Work and Academic experience

Start and finish dates

Reverse chronological order

Thesis: Only put thesis title if it is self-explanatory. Two line description of thesis. Do NOT put: exact date you defended you thesis (unless this is very recent); names of supervisors (unless they are known to the professor / company where you are applying, or are very famous in their field)

Work: Name of company, location, area of business. Academic: Name of department / institute, location

Your position in the company / lab / research group

Brief description of what you did, highlighting how it relates to the job you are applying for

Projects, publications and congresses - but if you have a lot of these (more than half a page), put in separate doc. If you are applying for a job in industry, just have a summary.

6.7 Languages

If the position you are applying for is in Europe: use the levels from the Common European Framework of Reference for Languages:

http://en.wikipedia.org/wiki/Common_European_Framework_of_Reference_for_Languages

Alternatively, put the results of any exams you have done e.g. TOEFL, ILETS, Cambridge.

Or use these terms: mother tongue; fluent (spoken and written); good working knowledge – means that you know enough to be able to carry out your work; scholastic.

6.8 Technical skills

Find out from the website of the institute / company what kind of technical skills that they are looking for – look at the descriptions of the tools (and equipment, methods, procedures, protocols) they use.

Try to find advertisements for jobs similar to the one you are looking for. Note the skills and qualities they want. If you have matching skills, put these first, then add any other skills that you think might be relevant.

If possible insert references to your technical skills under in the Work Experience and Academic Experience sections.

Imagine that these are the specifications for the position you are looking for

- Good knowledge of PQR
- Familiarity with XYZ
- Report writing skills
- Good communication skills

You can then write in your Work Experience section.

Worked in lab with PQR instrumentation. Drafted two requests for EU funding (both accepted). Attended three conferences on XYZ (one as an invited speaker). Trained new staff in ABC.

Note how each key point is mentioned: PQR, XYZ, drafted requests (= report writing), trained staff (= communication skills).

6.9   Communication skills

Do NOT list your communication skills. Instead, when referring to your work and academic experience, try to show that you have such skills.

Assistant researcher: worked on blah, blah, blah blah, blah using x, y, and z technologies. Successfully completed two projects on A and B, working to very tight deadlines. Responsible for small team of researchers. Held 3-month course for second-year undergraduates. Presented papers at two international conferences.

The example above demonstrates that you are responsible and can work under pressure (*tight deadlines*), you have leaderships skills (*team*), communication skills (*course*), writing skills and presentation skills (*presented papers*).

6.10   Personal interests / Other Information

These are important because they give an idea of your personality. This is the only part of the CV where you can really differentiate yourself from other candidates.

Be specific. Don't put things that most people probably do (eg reading, travelling). Don't write *sports*, instead write *swimming, hockey* etc.

Do not put activities that are political or contentious (eg hunting), but put things that are fun (eg salsa dancing) or interesting (eg acting). Avoid nerdy activities (computer games, collecting stamps) unless you know that the person reading your CV shares the same interests.

Not all institutes and companies require you to list your personal interests.

6.11   References

End your CV with a separate section entitled References, in which you list three or four people. These are people who can substantiate that what you have written in your CV is true. In the Anglosphere, employers often contact a candidate's references. For example:

Professor Adrian Wallwork (my thesis tutor), University of Manchester, a.wallwork@manuni.ac.uk

Professor Sara Cervello (in whose lab I did a 3-month internship), University of Harvard, s.cervello@harvard.edu

A 'reference' is a letter written by someone for whom you have worked or collaborated - typically your professor / tutor and people you have worked for during an internship. In this letter the professor gives a brief summary of your technical skills and also your personality (how motivated you are, how easy you are to work with, how proactive you are etc). You can attach this letter to your CV.

Whenever you work / collaborate with someone in a lab or a company, get a written reference from someone there. You can then use these references as and when you need them. Also, get permission from these people to put their names, position and email addresses on your CV.

6.11   References (cont.)

Some of the examples in this chapter have been taken from:

English for Academic CVs, Resumes, and Online Profiles

This book contains the following chapters:

1. Preliminaries - thinking about the type of job you want

2. Templates and Recruiters

3. Personal Information

4. Objectives and Personal Profiles

5. Personal Statements, Bios, and Publications

6. Education

7. Work Experience

8. Technical and soft skills

9. Personal Interests, Awards, Other Information

10. References and Reference Letters

11. Cover Letters

12. Checking your English and more ...

Chapter 7
Emails and Letters to the Editor

7.1 Salutations and general guidelines

Ten tips for writing effective emails

1. Meaningful subject line - otherwise recipient may not even open your mail.

2. Spell the person's name correctly - think how you feel when you see your own name is misspelled.

3. When writing the first time, use the full name that you find on the web - it may be difficult to establish someone's gender from their first name. The best solution is always to write both / all names (e.g. *Dear Stewart James, Dear Tao Pei Lin*).

4. Avoid *Mr, Mrs, Miss*, and *Ms*—they are not frequently used in emails. By NOT using them you avoid choosing the wrong one.

5. Never translate typical phrases literally - learn equivalent phrases.

6. Write the minimum amount possible - you will make fewer mistakes.

7. Always put the most important point in the first line - otherwise the reader may not see/read it.

8. Better to be a little too formal than too informal - you don't want to offend the recipient.

9. Always be polite - and remember if there is a minimal chance that your reader will misinterpret or be offended then you can be sure he/she will.

10. Limit your requests and questions – people will only respond regarding the easiest request or question. So limit yourself to the most important request. You can always send other requests in another email.

© The Author(s), under exclusive license to Springer Nature
Switzerland AG 2022
A. Wallwork, *Essential English Grammar and Communication Strategies*,
English for Academic Research, https://doi.org/10.1007/978-3-030-95612-7_7

7.1   Salutations and general guidelines (cont.)

Writing to someone for the FIRST time

The FIRST time you write to someone, for example, to me, you can write one of the three salutations below.

Dear Adrian Wallwork

Dear Dr Wallwork (I don't actually have a PhD, but I wouldn't be offended – nor would other recipients be offended unless they are professors)

Dear Professor Wallwork (I am not a university prof, but again I wouldn't be offended!)

The **SECOND** time (and future times) you write to someone you should only use one of the following forms:

Dear Dr/Prof Wallwork

Dear Adrian (if you know me well).

Do NOT write.

Dear Adrian Wallwork

Otherwise it sounds like this is the <u>first</u> time you are writing to me and that you have never made contact with them before.

If the person you are writing to is a similar age to you, then in your second email writing *Dear Adrian* would be absolutely appropriate.

7.1 Salutations and general guidelines (cont.)

Final salutation

Keep things short and simple (KISS principle). There are many ways to end an email, but you only need to learn one:

Best regards

You will never offend anyone if you finish your email simply with *Best regards*. Do not feel obliged to write additional salutations – what value do they add for your reader?

Replying to someone for the first time

- address them using exactly the same name (both first and last name) that they use in their signature

- precede this name with an appropriate title

- adopt their style and tone. If you are making the first contact, then it is safer to be formal in order to be sure not to offend anyone. Then as the relationship develops, you can become less (or more) formal as appropriate. In any case, always take into account the reader's customs and culture, remembering that some cultures are much more formal than others.

Being POLITE and FORMAL does NOT equal being respectful.

- Think ONLY about what your reader really needs to know - don't include information that is of interest to **you** but no interest to **him / her**.

- The reader is in a hurry – help them find what they want quickly and easily.

- Write **less and you make fewer mistakes.**

7.2 Email to understand status of your submitted paper

When you write an email, think first about what your desired outcome is. Then only write what will help you achieve that outcome. Always be constructive, positive and helpful.

Subject line: Paper submission- reply urgently!!

Dear Sir / Madam

My name is XX and I submitted my paper to you several months ago and I am still waiting for your judge.

This is the third email I write to know if my paper was admitted or not. Please answer me in any case.

Subject line: (1) *Manuscript 1453*

Dear (2) *Dear Editor / Dear Dr Helena Smith / Dear Dr Smith*

I was wondering (3) if you had received my email sent *date* (4) *see below*) regarding the submission of my manuscript (1453).

5) Please can you let me know if the review process has begun and when I can expect the reviewers' comments.

Attached is a 6) *copy of the paper for your convenience.*

Best regards

Key:

1. Write the subject line from their point of view, not yours. Give specific info.
2. Find out the editor's name, otherwise write *Dear Editor*
3. Use a polite neutral slight indirect expression – NOT a passive/aggressive approach.
4. Demonstrate any negative aspects indirectly rather than specifically referring to them. In this case you provide the evidence that you have been in contact several times before.
5. State what you want.
6. Be proactive.

Using the minimum number of words and a clear layout will increase the chances of your mail being read.

7.3 Email that contains constructive criticism

The email below was written to tell a colleague, with whom the writer was drafting a presentation. The writer felt that the colleague's first draft still needed working on.

I have carefully analysed your presentation and I believe that there are some serious shortcomings.

1) You need to do x.

2) You need to do y.

3) Please do z.

4) Also, I think you should do a and b.

Imagine that you receive the email above. How would you feel? A little angry, probably.

When criticizing, use this four-part structure:

1. Positive beginning – helps the reader accept the criticisms that you outline in stage 2

2. Constructive criticism

3. Offer solutions

4. Positive ending – reinforces the beginning and is designed to ensure your reader takes action

(1) Thanks for your presentation - I really liked some of the images you used, and the background template you have used is great.

2) I just have a couple of things to clarify …

Have you thought about doing x, y, z?

3) One thing we could do is … / The best solution might be ..

It might be a good idea if we … / Perhaps we could …

I have always found it useful to ...

If you like, I can try and do the Introduction.

4) Thanks for all the time you have spent on this - I really appreciate it.

With a few changes here and there, I think we can make a great presentation.

7.3 Email that contains constructive criticism (cont.)

Your aim is to achieve a goal (e.g. to produce a good presentation, to find out status of a paper submission). Your aim is **not** to humiliate the other person.

- You don't know the circumstances of the other person (maybe they have some personal problem at the moment).

- Maybe they sent you the wrong file (i.e. NOT the most recent version).

- Maybe they didn't have time to do what you were expecting them to do.

- Maybe they were imagining that you were going to do a particular task.

By helping the other person, you are also helping yourself – you both want the same outcome: a great presentation.

7.4 Writing a letter to the editor after the reviewers have asked for modifications to your paper

Imagine that you have sent your paper to a journal. The reviewers have read it and want you to i) check the English, ii) make a figure clearer, iii) add two references. The email below is an example of how NOT to reply.

Dear editor

I thought the paper was fine in terms of grammar and syntax, but as the reviewers noticed there were some mistakes, so I would like to know where they are in order to solve them and improve the paper.

Moreover you noticed that there were some problems in the figure too, would you mind to suggest me some advice to make them clearer?

To conclude I feel the references which you suggested don't fit completely, do you mind to explain why should I include them.

Kind regards,

The above email will only DELAY the publication of your paper. This is because you have asked a series of questions that will not only irritate the editor but which will entail him/her looking for answers – this takes time. The editor may decide not to answer. Moreover, there are several mistakes with the English

Below is an example of a good constructive email.

Please find attached the revised version of our paper entitled xxx (manuscript **No. 547646**).

We found the referees' suggestions **very useful** and have modified the manuscript accordingly.

- The English **has been checked** by a mother tongue professional editor.
- The figures **have been modified**, and made more concise.
- We **have included** the suggested bibliographic references.

We **hope** that you will find the revised manuscript suitable for publication.

Best regards

7.4 Writing a letter to the editor after the reviewers have asked for modifications to your paper (cont.)

The example above is good because:

- it makes the editor happy because you have done all that the referees required you to do
- there is a clear indication of which paper you are referring to (*manuscript No.*)
- it begins and ends in a positive way
- the English is correct - note the use of the present perfect to describe the changes you have made to the original version

When you receive the rebuttal letter there is a chance that you will not be happy, you will possibly be very angry. This is because what you THOUGHT was the perfect paper turns out not to be.

Your immediate reaction may be to write a rude email back immediately, stating how incompetent the reviewers are. This is a natural reaction and it is good to experience this reaction. But only experience it. Do not act on it. Instead leave the letter till tomorrow.

The next day re-read the report thinking about the reviewers not as incompetent imbeciles but as people who are actually trying to help you improve your paper. And by improving it, remember that more people are likely to read it and understand it.

Analyse the changes that the reviewers want. Do a cost–benefit analysis. For example if they ask you to adjust some figures and add some references, the cost to you of fulfilling these requirements is low. Changing the figures and references will NOT require much effort on your part – it is not important whether you agree or not that they need changing.

However, in some cases the cost would be high e.g. if they ask you to repeat an experiment.

Obviously, it's totally legitimate to disagree, but do so constructively. Show the editor you understand why the reviewer made a particular request / criticism.

7.4 Writing a letter to the editor after the reviewers have asked for modifications to your paper (cont.)

While we agree with the referee when he says that … nevertheless …

Yes, the referee is right in saying that x 0 Y. However ...

I understand why the referee might want … However ...

The rebuttal letter is spectacularly important.

- Essentially the editor just wants to check whether you have done what the reviewers requested. So where possible just write 'Done' and the line reference. This makes it much quicker for the editors to do their job.

- Rather than disputing what the referees say, do a cost / benefit analysis. Do what they ask if the cost to you is low.

- If you feel that you do not need or should not do what they ask, say why, but be constructive.

- Don't ask questions. You will just delay publication.

- Refrain from making any subjective comments or comments that might irritate the reviewers. At the same time you don't constantly need to say that you agree with the reviewers or that they are correct/right. Just write *done* (unless the journal specifies that you must explain every single you have made).

- Use *we* rather than 'the authors' - particularly when you are citing from the literature the editor may not know if you are talking about yourselves or the authors of other papers.

- Avoid informal language NO!! *Dear Editor, Thanks very much for the reviewer's great suggestions.*

- Adopting a friendly tone is unlikely to impress editors.

- Ensure the English is 100% correct – have it corrected.

7.4 Writing a letter to the editor after the reviewers have asked for modifications to your paper (cont.)

English for Interacting on Campus

Chapter 4 of this book is intended for university students and covers how to write emails to professors.

English for Academic Correspondence

This book covers how to write emails and letters in the world of academia. It contains the following chapters.

1. Subject Lines

2. Salutations

3. Structuring the content of an email

4. Building a Relationship and Deciding the Level of Formality

5. Language, Translating and Spelling

6. Requests and Replies

7. Cover letters for summer schools, internships, placements, Erasmus, PhD / MA / Postdoc programs

8. Reference letters

9. Brief notes on writing research proposals and research statements

10. How to criticize constructively

11. Writing a Peer Review

12. Writing a Reply to the Reviewers' Reports (*this is not an email, but is very important*)

13. Communicating with the Editor

14. Useful phrases

15. Tense Usage

Chapter 8
Link Words

8.1 about, as far as … is concerned, with regard to, regarding

All these expressions are used to introduce a topic.

Do not use **about** at the beginning of the sentence.

About the paper we sent you in May, we would like to know whether …

We are writing to you *about* the paper we sent you in May. We would like to

= *Concerning / regarding / on the subject of / with regard to* the paper we sent …

When the subject of *Concerning / regarding / on the subject of* etc is the same as the subject of the dependent clause, these expressions can often be avoided. This produces a more concise and readable sentence.

As far as the budget *is concerned*, this can be discussed at the next meeting.

With regard to telephone production, Nokia was once Europe's biggest producer of mobile units.

The budget can be discussed at the next meeting.

Nokia was once Europe's biggest producer of mobile telephones.

© The Author(s), under exclusive license to Springer Nature Switzerland AG 2022
A. Wallwork, *Essential English Grammar and Communication Strategies*, English for Academic Research, https://doi.org/10.1007/978-3-030-95612-7_8

8.1 about, as far as ... is concerned, with regard to, regarding (cont.)

Grammar Exercises: 5.20

8.2 also, in addition, further, furthermore, moreover

also, further, furthermore, in addition = additional positive or neutral comment

also is generally located before the main verb; the others are located at the beginning of the sentence

as well, but not **also**, is typically located at the end of the phrase.

She teaches French *also*.

In addition, she teaches French.

She *also* teaches French.

= She teaches French *as well*.

She teaches French *as well* as English.

This software program has several interesting features ... *In addition / Also / Furthermore*, the cost is low and it is quick to learn.

moreover = additional, typically negative, comment

This software program has *several interesting* features ... *Moreover*, the cost is low and it is quick to learn.

This software program has *several* interesting features. *In addition*, the cost is very high and it is quick to learn.

This software program has *very few* useful features. *Moreover*, the cost is very high and it is very difficult to learn.

8.2   also, in addition, further, furthermore, moreover (cont.)

Usage, Style, and Grammar: 13.2

Vocabulary Exercises: 2.2, 2.3

Writing Exercises: 4

8.3   because, why, due to, owing to, since

because – as a consequence

why – reason or explanation

Road safety is a fundamental issue *because* it helps to protect lives. That is *why* we have traffic lights and ...

Our aim was to find out *why* organizing teachers' timetables is such a time-consuming process.

The students failed the exam. This was *because* they hadn't studied and this is also *why* they will have to retake it.

There are three reasons *why* this is important.

due to and **owing to** mean the same as **because of**, and are followed by a noun.

owing to tends only to be used at the beginning of a sentence.

due to the fact that and **owing to the fact that** are used before a subject + verb construction.

This battery may explode when used with a third-party power supply. This is *due to the fact* that the battery is highly inflammable and this is *the reason [why]* it should not be used in children's toys.

As / Since / Given that / On account of the fact that they wanted total control, the revolutionary party enacted a series of drastic reforms.

This accident was *due to* an electrical fault = *Owing to* an electrical fault there was an accident.

Due to / As a result of / On account of its toxicity, this substance cannot be used.

Due to the fact that / Owing to the fact that we only had a limited budget, it was decided to use the cheapest version.

Usage, Style, and Grammar: 13.8

Vocabulary Exercises: 2.11

8.4   both, either, neither

both = A + B

neither ... nor = not A, not B

not ... either = not A, not B

either ... or = just A or just B, but only <u>one</u> of the two

Both of the experiments *did not produce* the expected results.

Both the two procedures are taken from Yin et al. (2022).

Students can study *both* English *or* Spanish, i.e. they only have the option to study one of them.

Students can study *either* Russian *or* Korean, i.e. two languages.

Students *cannot* study *neither* Russian *and* Korean, just one of the two.

Neither of the experiments *produced* the expected results.

Both the procedures are taken from Yin et al. (2022).

Students can study *either* English *or* Spanish, i.e. they only have the option to study one of them.

Students <u>cannot</u> study *both* Russian *and* Korean, i.e. they can only study one language.

Students <u>can</u> study *both* Russian *and* Korean, i.e. they can study two languages.

Usage, Style, and Grammar: 13.3, 13.9

Vocabulary Exercises: 2.12, 2.13

Writing Exercises: 13.9

8.5 even if, even though, although

even if - hypothetical situations (often used with *would*)

Even if you gave me a million dollars I would never lie in court. = You will never give me a million dollars.

Even if we had all the time in the world, we would never be able to finish the project. = We do not have all the time in the world.

although, even though - real situations (often used with simple present)

Even though / Although she is English she does not support the royal family. = She <u>is</u> English.

Even though / Although they live next door, I never see them. = They <u>are</u> my neighbors.

Even if it was really hot they wore a coat.

Her English is not very good *even* she has studied it for ten years.

I prefer red wine to white wine, *even if* I enjoy white wine too.

Even though it was really hot, they wore a coat.

Her English is not very good *even though* she has studied it for ten years.

I prefer red wine to white wine, *although* I enjoy white wine too.

Usage, Style, and Grammar: 13.14

Vocabulary Exercises: 2.4

Writing Exercises: 14.16

8.6   the former, the latter

the former – the first of one or more items mentioned in the previous sentence

the latter – the last of the items mentioned in the previous sentence

Example:

Two countries are involved in this project: <u>Cambodia</u> and **Laos**. <u>The former</u> has a population of 16.5 million, **the latter** just over 7 million.

When you refer back to something you mentioned before, it is often not immediately clear what *the former* and *the latter* refer to. Example:

Africa has a greater population than the combined populations of Russia, Canada and the United States. In *the latter* the population is only ...

In the sentence above, does *the latter* refer just to the US alone, or to the US and Canada? The simplest and clearest solution is to replace the latter with the exact word or words it refers to. This gives:

Africa has a greater population than the combined populations of Russia, Canada and the United States. *In the USA* the population is only ...

Africa has a greater population than the combined populations of Russia, Canada and the United States. In *Canada and the USA* the population is only ...

It is ALWAYS better to repeat words if the result is that the reader will be clear about what you want to say.

Usage, Style, and Grammar: 13.13, 15.14

100 Tips to Avoid Mistakes: 41

Grammar mistakes: 6.1

8.7   however, although, but, yet, despite

however,   although,   but,   yet,   despite,   nevertheless,   nonetheless, notwithstanding

All these words have a very similar meaning. Below are just the ones that are used the most frequently.

You do not need to use the other ones. In fact, it is best NOT use them as some involve complicated grammatical rules.

however, but - to qualify what you have just written (*but* is less formal). *however* is used in preference to *but* at the beginning of a sentence. *however* can be used with or without a comma, and can be located mid phrase between two commas.

yet - the same as *but* and *however*, but has a stronger note of surprise.

although - often used to qualify a statement. NOT used a) between commas, b) directly before a verb, c) at the end of a phrase.

The system costs very little to implement, *despite / notwithstanding* it is very complicated to use.

Governments know this is a problem, *despite* they do nothing about it.

Despite the cost is cheap, the system is very effective.

The system costs very little to implement, *but / however / yet / although* it is very complicated to use.

= The system costs very little to implement. *However*, it is very complicated to use.

= The system costs very little to implement. It is, *however*, very complicated to use.

Governments know this is a problem, *yet* they do nothing about it.

= *Although* governments know this is a problem, they still do nothing about it.

Although it is very cheap, the system is very effective.

= The system is cheap, *yet / however / but* it is very effective.

8.7   however, although, but, yet, despite (cont.)

Usage, Style, and Grammar: 13.14, 13.15

Vocabulary Exercises: 2.17

Writing Exercises: 4.10

8.8   instead, on the other hand, whereas, on the contrary

instead - beginning of a sentence; introduces resolution to a problem stated in the previous sentence. Not used to introduce a new topic.

on the other hand - gives alternative or additional information about something mentioned previously. *whereas* is not used in such circumstances. Do not use *on the other hand* to introduce new information without any sense of contrast.

on the other hand and **whereas** introduce a contrast to what has just been stated; use *whereas* for a stronger contrast.

Do not join two independent clauses with a semicolon. *On the other hand*, make two simple separate sentences.

The conference may be held in Jordon, *whereas* it may be held in Egypt.

This year the conference is being held in Prague, *on the other hand* last year it was held on the other side of the globe in Sydney.

Italian and Spanish are similar languages. *Whereas* German is completely different.

Do not join two independent clauses with a semicolon. *Instead*, make two simple separate sentences.

The conference may be held in Jordon, *on the other hand* it may be held in Egypt.

This year the conference is being held in Prague, *whereas* last year it was held on the other side of the globe in Sydney.

Italian and Spanish are similar languages, *whereas* German is completely different.

We found that x = 1, *whereas [on the other hand]* Smith et al reached a very different conclusion that x = 2.

on the contrary - only to totally contradict what another author has stated

8.8 instead, on the other hand, whereas, on the contrary (cont.)

Do not join two independent clauses with a semicolon. *On the contrary*, make two simple separate sentences.

Smith [2023] states that governments must intervene in such cases. We believe, *on the other hand*, that they absolutely must not intervene.

Do not join two independent clauses with a semicolon. *Instead*, make two simple separate sentences.

Smith [2023] states that governments must intervene in such cases. We believe, *on the contrary*, that they absolutely must not intervene.

Usage, Style, and Grammar: 13.17

Vocabulary Exercises: 2.21

Writing Exercises: 4.16

8.9   thus, therefore, hence, consequently, so

thus, therefore, consequently, so and **hence** all indicate a consequence of what has just been said before

thus is the most commonly used, and is often found before the main verb, rather than at the beginning of the sentence

consequently is often used at the beginning of a sentence, separated by a comma

hence is generally reserved for mathematics

so is considered informal and inappropriate for academic writing

Researchers do not have much time to read papers. *Consequently*, it makes sense to write papers in a way that they can understand quickly and easily. = It *thus* makes sense ...

Note that the right-hand side of equation (2) equals r(p)v(x)+[3]. *Hence*, equation (2) reduces to equation (1) if ... = equals r(p)v(x)+[3], *thus* equation (1) reduces to an ordinary linear equation.

Note the use of *thus* with the *-ing* form (see 13.3).

Love promotes good mental health *enabling* people to live better lives.

Love promotes good mental health *thus* enabling people to live better lives.

= Love promotes well-being. The consequence of this well-being is that people can live better lives.

Usage, Style, and Grammar: 13.18

Vocabulary Exercises: 2.9, 2.15

Writing Exercises: 4.6

8.10   which, who vs. that

which: adds extra information to the previous phrase. **which** is usually preceded by a comma

who: refers to people only and is used to add extra information

that: defines the concept given in the previous phrase. **that** is NOT preceded by a comma

Correct the sentences below, *that* contain grammatical mistakes.

1) Correct the sentences below, *which* contain grammatical mistakes. = Students are instructed to correct ALL the sentences below. Students are informed that the sentences contain grammatical mistakes (not, for example, vocabulary mistakes).

2) The sentences below, which all contain grammatical mistakes, must be corrected = Same meaning as previous sentence.

3) Correct the sentences below that contain grammatical mistakes. = Students are instructed to correct ONLY those sentences that contain grammatical mistakes. This means that some of the sentences do not contain mistakes.

Given that not many people are aware of this distinction (**which** – additional info, **that** – restrictive), it is better to rewrite the sentences more explicitly.

Sentence 1: Correct the sentences below, <u>all of which</u> contain grammatical mistakes.

Sentence 3: Correct <u>only</u> those sentences below that contain grammatical mistakes.

which, **that** and **who** (for people) should only refer to the noun that immediately precedes them.

8.10   which, who vs. that (cont.)

A group of patients was compiled using this procedure, as proposed by Smith and Jones [2024], who had died under surgery.

In the sentence above it seems that Smith and Jones died under surgery! This ambiguity arises because the subject (*patients*) has been separated from its verb (*had died*) by a subordinate clause (*as proposed* ...). The solution is to keep the subject and verb as close as possible to each other.

A group of patients who had died under surgery was compiled using this procedure, as proposed by Smith and Jones [2024].

In any case, when using *which* and *who*, be sure it is clear what *which* or *who* refer to.

Usage, Style, and Grammar: 7.1, 7.2

Grammar Exercises: 5.1, 5.2, 5.5, 5.6

Writing Exercises: 6.2

Chapter 9
Paragraphs, Paraphrasing, Sentence Length

9.1 Paragraphs

In the early 1960s, a senior staff scientist at NASA, was concerned that the documents that were written by NASA engineers were NOT very clear – even though they were written by native speakers for native speakers! The scientist, Sam Katzoff, thus decided to write a short pamphlet entitled 'Clarity in Technical Reporting'. The first paragraph is reported below. The rest of this section analyses how the paragraph is constructed.

Different writers have different methods of organizing their reports, and some seem to have no discernible method at all. Most of the better writers, however, appear to be in remarkably close agreement as to the general approach to organization. This approach consists of stating the problem, describing the method of attack, developing the results, discussing the results, and summarizing the conclusions. You may feel that this type of organization is obvious, logical, and natural. Nevertheless, it is not universally accepted. For example, many writers present results and conclusions near the beginning, and describe the derivation of these results in subsequent sections.

First sentence: introduces overall topic

Different writers have different methods of organizing their reports, and some seem to have no discernible method at all.

Sentences are linked together - an idea from one sentence is recalled in the next sentence

Different writers have different methods of organizing their reports, and some seem to have no discernible method at all. Most of the **better writers**, however, appear to be in remarkably close agreement as to the general **approach** to **organization**. This **approach** consists of stating the problem, describing the method of attack, developing the results, discussing the results, and summarizing the conclusions. You may feel that this type of **organization** is obvious, logical, and natural.

A. Wallwork, *Essential English Grammar and Communication Strategies*, English for Academic Research, https://doi.org/10.1007/978-3-030-95612-7_9

9.1   Paragraphs (cont.)

Maximum of <u>two</u> ideas per sentence

You may feel that this type of organization is obvious, logical, and natural. **(one idea)**

Nevertheless, it is not universally accepted. **(one idea)**

For example, many writers present results and conclusions near the beginning, and describe the derivation of these results in subsequent sections. **(two ideas)**

Vary the length of sentences

You may feel that this type of organization is obvious, logical, and natural. Nevertheless, it is not universally accepted. **(6 words)**

For example, many writers present results and conclusions near the beginning, and describe the derivation of these results in subsequent sections. **(21 words)**

Repeating key words is OK

Different **writers** have different methods of organizing their reports, and some seem to have no discernible method at all. Most of the better **writers**, however, appear to be in remarkably close agreement as to the general approach to organization. .. Nevertheless, it is not universally accepted. For example, many **writers** present results and conclusions near the beginning, and describe the derivation of these results in subsequent sections.

Don't use different words to mean the same key concept. If the NASA scientist had used *writer* in the first case, *author* in the second, and *researcher* in the third, then the reader might have thought that *writer, author, researcher* were three different types of people, rather than being exactly the same person.

If you are talking about a test, and then refer to this test later, do NOT call it an *experiment* or *trial*. If you are referring to gold, always call it *gold*, NOT *this metal* or *this precious item*.

Just choose ONE word, and always use that word.

9.1 Paragraphs (cont.)

The scientists and engineers who work at NASA are among the most intelligent people in the world. They <u>can</u> understand long complex sentences. But they decide to use short simple sentences and paragraphs in the documents that they write for each other. You should do the same.

Your English instructor's joy at your ability to compose grammatically correct 200-word sentences must be disregarded as against your present goal of simplifying your reader's job.

Sam Katzoff, author of the NASA document "Clarity in Technical Reporting"

Clarity in Technical Reporting by S Katzoff (NASA Scientific and Technical Information Division) is freely available at: http://courses.media.mit.edu/2010spring/mas111/NASA-64-sp7010.pdf

I would like to thank NASA's Office of Communication for allowing me to quote freely from Katzoff's article.

English for Writing Research Papers (2016 edn.): Chapter 3. See 3.17 for a full analysis of the NASA paragraph.

100 Tips to Avoid Mistakes: 63

9.2   Paraphrasing and Plagiarism

Plagiarism means cutting and pasting from other studies and papers – including your own. Some journals stipulate that you cannot use more than five consecutive words from another paper that you have written. Journals also use software to scan your paper for evidence of plagiarism. If there is plagiarism, then your paper may initially be rejected.

One way to avoid plagiarism is to paraphrase what others (or you in another paper) have said. However you still need to acknowledge the source of the original idea or result by putting a reference to the place where the original statement was made.

Let's look at ways to paraphrase the quotation below by Robert Heinlein (1907-1988), who was a science fiction author and engineer. [Note the date of 1956 is invented as I was unable to find the exact date he wrote / said this]

Everything is theoretically impossible, until it is done. (Heinlein, 1956)

Heinlein (1956) proposed the 'everything is theoretically impossible, until it is done'.

Synonyms

Heinlein (1956) proposed / suggested / stated / found / contended that nothing is possible until it is actually carried out.

Nothing is possible until it is actually carried out, according to Heinlein.

Active to passive

It has been proposed / suggested / stated / found / contended that until researchers carry out an activity, that activity is in theory impossible (Heinlein, 1956).

Different form, Different word order

According to (Heinlein, 1956), until an experiment is made it cannot be proved that something is possible.

For something to be proved, rather than just theorized, an experiment has to be conducted (Heinlein, 1956).

9.2 Paraphrasing and Plagiarism (cont.)

Paraphrasing avoids:

- Plagiarism

- Repetition of phrases within your paper

- Mistakes – if you are not 100% sure of what you have written, paraphrase it (generally by simplifying)

English for Writing Research Papers (2016 edn.), Chapter 11

9.3   Sentence length

Guidelines on sentence length

Write your first draft without thinking too much about the length of the sentences. Then look for long sentences and read them aloud. If you have to inhale, you need to divide up the sentence.

- Do NOT write a <u>series</u> of sentences of only 5-15 words.

- Occasionally use short sentences to attract attention (particularly in the Abstract and Discussion).

- <u>Generally speaking</u>, avoid sentences of more than 35 words.

However, clarity and readability are independent of sentence length. You <u>can</u> write a long sentence and still be clear. Also, a short sentence will not, by definition, necessarily be clear. Prioritize clarity above everything else.

Your main aim is to maintain readers' interest so that they continue reading (or listening).

A series of long sentences is generally not an acceptable form of writing

The two sentences below come from the introduction of an English Grammar written 200 years ago by Lindley Murray, an American grammarian. The first sentence contains 59 words, the second 79 words. Such sentences were common and acceptable 200 years ago, even 50 years ago. But not now! Try to keep your sentences below 30 words, unless these sentences contain lists of examples.

When the number and variety of English Grammars already published, and the ability with which some of them are written, are considered, little can be expected from a new compilation, besides a careful selection of the most useful matter, and some degree of improvement in the mode of adapting it to the understanding, and the gradual progress of learners. ... ... The more important rules, definitions, and observations, and which are therefore the most proper to be committed to memory, are printed with a larger type; whilst rules and re- marks that are of less consequence, that extend or diversify the general idea, or that serve as explanations, are contained in the smaller letter: these, or the chief off them, will be perused by the student to the greatest ad- vantage, if postponed till the general system be completed.

9.3 Sentence length (cont.)

If you want people to read what you have written, then you need to make it easy for them. You can do this by writing short sentences (but not EVERY sentence needs to be short!).

You may find examples still today of native English-speaking academics who regularly use long sentences. Although in my opinion their approach is not ideal, at least they have the advantage of not making mistakes with the language. The combination of long sentences AND mistakes with the English, is likely to encourage your readers to stop reading. And if they stop reading, all the time you spent on your research will be wasted.

How to keep your sentences short

Examples of two very simple sentence with one part and two parts:

English is often considered to be the simplest language.

Of all the languages in the world, English is often considered to be the simplest.

Avoid the following three mistakes, which are highlighted in the red sentences below.

1. The key information should NOT be placed in the *middle* of the sentence.

2. Don't put the <u>subject</u> too far from the <u>key information</u>

3. Don't hide the subject in the middle of the phrase

1) English, *which is the international language of communication*, is now studied by 1.1 billion people.

1) English, *which is now studied by 1.1 billion people*, is the international language of communication.

2) English, which owes its origins to the Anglo Saxons (a tribe who lived in what is now Denmark and Northern Germany) and is the international language of communication, in part due to the importance of the USA, rather than the King of England, is now studied by 1.1 billion people.

9.3   Sentence length (cont.)

3) Owing to its origins to the Anglo Saxons (a tribe who lived in what is now Denmark and Northern Germany), English is the international language of communication, in part due to the importance of the USA, rather than GB, and is now studied by 1.1 billion people.

Solution: Divide up the sentence into smaller parts.

English owes its origins to the Anglo Saxons, who were a tribe from what is now Denmark and Northern Germany. // It has become the international language of communication. // This is in part due to the importance of the USA, rather than GB. // English is now studied by 1.1 billion people.

Good places to start a new sentence

PARENTHESES

Either remove them and leave the text, or remove both the parentheses AND the text.

English, which owes its origins to the Anglo Saxons *(a tribe who lived in what is now Denmark and Northern Germany)*.

English owes its origins to the Anglo Saxons, a tribe who lived in what is now Denmark and Northern Germany.

English owes its origins to the Anglo Saxons.

9.3   Sentence length (cont.)

INTERVENING OR RELATIVE CLAUSE (... , *WHICH* , ...)

English, *which owes its origins to the Anglo Saxons,* is ...

English owes its origins to the Anglo Saxons.

A SERIES OF *AND's* OR OTHER LINK WORDS, CONSIDER BEGINNING A NEW SENTENCE
WHERE THE LINK WORDS IS LOCATED

.... a tribe who lived in what is now Denmark and northern Germany, *and is the*
international language of communication,

.... a tribe who lived in what is now Denmark and northern Germany. English is the
international language of communication,

A LOT OF COMMAS

English is the international language of communication, *in part* due to the importance of the USA, rather than the King of England, *is* now studied by 1.1 billion people.

English is the international language of communication and is now studied by 1.1
billion people. This is in part due to the importance of the USA, rather than the King
of England.

9.3   Sentence length (cont.)

Having shorter sentences makes it easier to change their order

Short sentences not only help your reader. They also help your co-authors. If you are responsible for writing the first draft and you present your co-authors with a manuscript full of long sentences, it will be very hard work for them to modify your texts or move words and sentences around. Instead, they will probably make an already long sentence even longer! A much better approach is to present your co-authors with a text that is relatively simple to modify. This means that your co-authors can add/cut words and phrases, change the sequence of phrases etc.

The example below shows how short sentence can be moved around easily.

English owes its origins to the Anglo Saxons, who were a tribe from what is now Denmark and Northern Germany. // English has become the international language of communication. // This is in part due to the importance of the USA, rather than GB. // English is now studied by 1.1 billion people.

English is now studied by 1.1 billion people. It owes its origins to the Anglo Saxons, who were a tribe from what is now Denmark and Northern Germany. // English has become the international language of communication. // This is in part due to the importance of the USA, rather than GB.

English for Writing Research Papers (2016 edn.), Chapter 4

Chapter 10
Prepositions and Adverbs

10.1 above (below), over (under)

above and **below** - paragraphs, figures and tables etc

above and **below** - levels, lists, averages and hierarchies

over has a similar meaning to *cover*, i.e. there is often physical contact between two elements

With numbers, **over** = more than, and **under** = less than

The figure *below* shows ...

As mentioned *above* there are three main methods, which are summarized in the table *below*.

A full professor is *above* an assistant professor in the academic hierarchy.

A sheet was placed *over* the patient's body.

Athens is between 70 m and 380 m *above* sea level which is *below* the national average for Greek cities.

Only children *over* the age of 13 were considered in the sample. Those *under* 12 years of age will be the subject of a future investigation.

above all = the most important thing

overall = globally

10.1   above (below), over (under) (cont.)

Several points need to be considered, *above all* age and sex.

Overall, our results are an important step towards finding a cure for this disease.

Vocabulary Exercises: 4.2

10.2 among, between, of, from

between = two different items or groups of two or more distinct items

among = a number of indistinct items

of = before an indeterminate number of the same item

from = after a verb when making a selection (*choose from, pick from, select from*)

from ... to / and = for a range

Many men cannot distinguish *among* red and green.

Unemployment *between* graduates is estimated at higher than 40%.

Vietnam lies *among* China, Cambodia and Laos.

Tomorrow's temperature will vary *between* 20 *to* 25 degrees.

Many men cannot distinguish *between* red and green.

Unemployment *among* graduates is estimated at higher than 40%.

Vietnam lies *between* China, Cambodia and Laos.

Tomorrow's temperature will vary *between* 20 and 25 degrees. / vary *from* 20 *to* 25 degrees.

10.2   among, between, of, from (cont.)

Instead of using **between, among** and **of** at the beginning of the sentence, consider rearranging the sentence.

Among / Of the possible biological fluids, peripheral blood is one of the most studied.

Peripheral blood is one of the most studied biological fluids.

Usage, Style, and Grammar: 14.4

Vocabulary Exercises: 4.3, 4.4

10.3   as is *vs* as it is

as (is): when referring to a figure, diagram, table, previous paragraph / section, or to what someone else has written

as it: ONLY when you are giving an explanation. The meaning is the same as: *because, since, given that*

As it can be seen from Table 1, the values are ...

This is not true, *as it* is evident from the figure.

As it is mentioned above, we were unable to ...

As can been seen from Table 1, the values are ...

This is not true, *as is* evident from the figure.

This is not true, *as / because* it is impossible to prove that X=Y.

As mentioned above and *as* can be seen in the figure, we were unable to ...

As stated by Marchesi et al (2023), there is no reason to believe that ...

Usage, Style, and Grammar: 13.6

Vocabulary Exercises: 2.7

10.4 as vs like (unlike), such as

as - in the role of

like - similar to but not the real thing; in the same way as

Nadine is acting *as* project leader while Amaja is away. = Nadine has become a temporary project leader.

Nadine acts *like* a project leader. = She dresses smart, gives people orders etc – but she is not the project leader.

Diabetes acts *as* a significant risk factor for many physical diseases. = Diabetes is a risk factor.

Xerostima: A symptom that acts *like* a disease. = Xerostima, i.e. dry mouth resulting from absent saliva flow, is not a disease but a symptom that can lead to a disease.

Like can be seen in the table, the values are considerably lower this time.

Like a prototype it worked well, but not in its final version.

It behaves *as* the other one.

It can be used *like* an alternative.

As can be seen in the table, the values are considerably lower this time.

As a prototype it worked well, but not in its final version.

It behaves *like* the other one.

It can be used *as* an alternative.

10.4   as vs like (unlike), such as (cont.)

the same + as

(not) as ... as: to make comparisons highlighting that two things are (not) equal

such as = for example

unlike: to make a contrast

Several countries, *as* Ivory Coast, Senegal and Zimbabwe, have adopted this new approach.

Lead behaves *as* copper and iron.

Zinc, *differently from* copper and iron, fails to stimulate lipid peroxidation in vitro.

Zinc does not behave in the *same way than* copper and iron.

Several countries, *such as* Ivory Coast, Senegal and Zimbabwe, have adopted this new approach.

Lead behaves in the *same way as* copper and iron.

Zinc, *unlike* copper and iron, fails to stimulate lipid peroxidation in vitro.

Zinc does not behave *in the same way as* copper and iron.

Usage, Style, and Grammar: 13.7

Vocabulary Exercises: 2.8

10.5 at, in, into, to (location, state, change)

at + buildings and workplace

in + towns, countries etc. No movement is involved

into when movement is involved

to after a verb that indicates a destination

at when describing the location of items in diagrams and figures

in before figures, tables etc when used in association with verbs such as *see, show, highlight*

We found the book *into* the box.

They are *into* the garden.

The bar has been transformed *in* a restaurant.

They arrived *to* the airport while we were still *to* work and Karl was *to* the restaurant.

We found the book *in* the box.

We put the item *into / in* the box.

They are *in* the garden.

The bar has been transformed *into* a restaurant.

They arrived *at* the airport, while we were still *at* work and Karl was *at* the restaurant.

They arrived *in* New York, while we were still *in* China.

They have gone *to* Beirut for a conference.

This can be seen *at* the top / bottom / side / edge of the figure.

As can be seen *in* Figure 1, the trend is ... Also, as highlighted *in* Table 3 ...

This was then moved *to* the top / bottom of the list.

10.5   at, in, into, to (location, state, change) (cont.)

to with these verbs: *adhere, adjust, attach, attract, bind, bring, come, confine, conform, connect, consign, convey, deliver, direct, email, fax, go, lead, link, move, react, reply, respond, restrict, send, stick, supply, switch, take, tend, tie, transmit, write, yield.* This rule also applies to the related nouns: *delivery, modification, response, tendency* etc

to with these adjectives: *adjacent, close, contingent, contiguous, external, internal, next, orthogonal, parallel, perpendicular, tangent, transverse*

in with: *equilibrium, parallel, series*

I do not adhere *to* these principles.

My house is adjacent *to* hers.

The three forces shown in the diagram are *in* equilibrium.

Usage, Style, and Grammar: 14.5

Vocabulary Exercises: 4.5-4.7

108

10.6   at, in, on (time, measurement, quality)

at + a time of day, and with specific periods (*the weekend, Easter, Christmas*)

in + a period of time (*week, month, year, decade, century* etc), including historical periods (*in the Middle Ages, in the Renaissance* etc)

on + a day. Note some native speakers say *on the weekend* others *at the weekend*

The meeting is scheduled to start *at* 15.30.

The conference will be held *in* June.

I will contact you *on* Monday morning.

We usually take our holidays *at* Easter or *at* Christmas, and of course *at* the weekend.

The last conference on this topic was held *in* 2024 and the previous one *in* the 2010s. The first was held *in* the 18th century.

We do not work *on* Christmas Day, *on* Easter day and *on* July 4 (Independence Day).

at with *degree, interval, level, node, point, pressure, ratio, speed, stage, temperature, velocity*

to with these verbs: *approximate, calculate, correct, heat, measure, raise*

to with these adjectives: *inferior, superior; equal, identical, proportional, similar; immune, impermeable, open, resistant, sensitive; according, alternative, analogous, attention, common, comparable, identical, inferior, likened, open, opposed, proportional, relative, relevant, responsive, similar, suited, superior, transparent*

to with these nouns: *conformance, compliance, correspondence, entitlement*

Water boils *at* a temperature of 100 C.

Heat the water *to* a temperature of 50 C.

The vehicle moves *at* a velocity / speed of 300 cm/h.

The potassium content was approximated *to* 90 mEq/kg.

Gender is common *to* all Latinate languages, but has no adherence *to* logical rules.

10.6 at, in, on (time, measurement, quality) (cont.)

Usage, Style, and Grammar: 14.5

Vocabulary Exercises: 4.5-4.7

10.7 by *vs* from (cause, means and origin)

by – agent (the person or thing that does something)

from - origin or source of something

The manuscript has now been revised *from* a native English speaker.

We received a letter of acceptance *by* the editor.

The original computers were made *from* IBM.

This mixture is made *by* a variety of substances from all over the world.

Taxes were raised *from* the government.

The manuscript has now been revised *by* a native English speaker.

We received a letter of acceptance *from* the editor = the editor sent us a letter.

The original computers were made *by* IBM.

This mixture is made *from* a variety of substances / is made *up of* a variety of substances.

Taxes were raised *by* the government.

from with these verbs: *arise, benefit, borrow, deduce, defend, deviate, differ, ensue, exclude, originate, profit, protect, release, remove, select, separate, shield, subtract, suffer*

from with these nouns that derive from the verbs listed above: *deviation, exclusion, protection*

The economic crisis arose *from* banking malpractices and indiscriminate consumer-borrowing *from* banks.

Considerable damage was caused *by* the earthquake.

This paper suffers *from* a lack of detailed discussion and would also benefit *from* a complete revision of the English.

10.7   by *vs* from (cause, means and origin) (cont.)

Note: *depend on, subtract from, multiply by*

The number was then divided or multiplied *by* 32.5, depending *on* the case.

The corresponding amount was obtained *by* subtracting the first value *from* the second.

Usage, Style, and Grammar: 14.10

Vocabulary Exercises: 4.8

10.8   by, in, of (changes)

When reporting increases, decreases, modifications, changes, variations etc, use:

by after a verb

of before a number

in before a noun

A fall *in* unemployment is predicted.

Attendance has fallen *by* 16%.

The stock market has risen *by* 213 points.

There has been an increase *in* inflation *of* 5%.

There has been a 5% increase *in* inflation.

This was affected by variations *of* 16% and more.

Usage, Style, and Grammar: 14.11

Vocabulary Exercises: 4.9

10.9   currently, to date, until now, so far

currently = now, at present + PRESENT SIMPLE AND PRESENT CONTINUOUS

to date, **until now** and **so far** = from a certain point in the past up to the present moment and possibly in the near future too + PRESENT PERFECT

For the position of **currently, to date, until now** and **so far** in a phrase see the example phrases below and see also 14.7.

These terms are rarely used in manuscripts.

actually = in reality; *presently* = after a short time (it is rarely used in academia)

till = very informal version of until, not used in academia

There are *actually / presently* three approaches to this problem.

So far / Until now, research into this area *is* limited to X.

This is the only acid that *so far / until now is* found to be effective in such scenarios.

The research *to date* undertaken has only focused on ...

Till now no solution has been found.

There are *currently* three approaches to this problem.

So far / Until now, research into this area *has been* limited to X. In this paper, we investigate Y.

This is the only acid that *has* so *far / until* now *been found* to be effective in such scenarios.

To date, the research undertaken *has only focused* on ... = The research undertaken *to date* has ...

The research undertaken *so far / until* now has only focused on ...

Until now, no solution has been found. = There is currently no solution.

10.9 currently, to date, until now, so far (cont.)

Usage, Style, and Grammar: 14.6

Vocabulary Exercises: 1.2, 1.13

10.10   during, over, throughout

during = at some point in the course of a period of time. This period can either be in the past or future

over = period of time that began in the past and is still true in the present + PRESENT PERFECT

However, *over* can also be used for a future period e.g. *over the next few years*

throughout means for the entire course of a period of time (past, present or future)

I hope to have the opportunity of meeting you *during* the conference next month.

I worked with him *during* my Erasmus project.

Over the last few years, there has been increasing interest in ... = For the last few years, i.e. until and including today

Over the last decade, no progress has been made in ... However, over the next few years this will certainly change.

Throughout history, humans have had a tendency to collect objects - even objects of no apparent value.

Plagues were common *throughout* the Middle Ages.

Usage, Style, and Grammar: 14.14

Vocabulary Exercises: 4.10

10.11   for, since, from (time)

for = period that began in the past and continues into the present. Typically used with plural words indicating time, e.g. *days, months, years, decades*.

for answers the question 'how long has this situation been ongoing?' In this sense, *for* + PRESENT PERFECT.

since = starting point of a current situation. Typically used with precise points in time, e.g. *2022, last month, yesterday* + PRESENT PERFECT

since answers the question 'when did this situation begin?'

from = a range of time, i.e. with a start and finish. Because there is a finish time, *from* is not used with the PRESENT PERFECT. But *from* can be used with most other tenses.

We *do* this research *from / since* nine years.

Over the last few months there *is* a lot of media coverage.

I *have studied* in Boston *for* three years and then I *have moved* to Beijing.

From / Since 2021 there is a dramatic increase in cases.

I have studied in Boston from 2019 to 2022.

We *have been doing* this research *for* nine years.

Over the last few months *there has been* a lot of media coverage.

I *studied* in Boston *for* three years and then I *moved* to Beijing.

Since 2001 there *has been* a dramatic increase in cases.

I *studied* in Boston from 2019 to 2022.

10.11   for, since, from (time) (cont.)

Other expressions denoting a duration from past to present are: **over** (e.g. over the last two decades), **so far, to date, until now**

If *for* indicates a period of time that is now finished + SIMPLE PAST

Note: *few* is required in the following types of expressions:

For the last *few* decades, researchers have been in interested in ...

The last *few* years have witnessed an increase in interest in ...

Usage, Style, and Grammar: 14.13, 14.15

Grammar Exercises: 6.2

Vocabulary Exercises: 1.34, 2.14

Chapter 11
Present and Past Tenses Used in Research Papers

11.1 Guidelines

Below are some guidelines on the use of the three most common tenses in research papers: PRESENT SIMPLE, PRESENT PERFECT, PAST SIMPLE. These guidelines are NOT grammatical rules. The guidelines can be broken. They vary depending on the author, the discipline, and the journal.

In all the guidelines, I have indicated which sections of the paper (Abstract, Introduction, Methods, Results, Discussion, Conclusions) the guidelines typically refer to.

I only focus on the Present Simple, Present Perfect and Past Simple, as these three tenses are the most frequently used in research papers. I also mention the Present Continuous.

cf = compare. Sometimes in square brackets I give an example of another tense in order to highlight the difference between the two tenses.

For guidelines on the other tenses:

all tenses used in various sections of a paper	**Grammar Exercises**: 19-25
conditionals	**Usage 9.1.9.5, Grammar Exercises**: 9
future forms	**Usage 8.10, Grammar Exercises**: 8
modal verbs	**Usage 12.1-12.8, Grammar Exercises**: 12
past continuous and past perfect	**Usage 8-9, Grammar Exercises**: 7.7-7.9
present perfect continuous	**Usage 8.8, Grammar Exercises**: 7.4

For a general overview of the grammar used in other areas of communication (i.e. not just research papers), see Chapter 15 in *English for Interacting on Campus*.

A. Wallwork, *Essential English Grammar and Communication Strategies*, English for Academic Research, https://doi.org/10.1007/978-3-030-95612-7_11

11.2   All sections of a paper

Facts – PRESENT SIMPLE

Smoking *kills* around eight million people a year.

The richest 10% of the world's population *own* 85% of global assets.

It *is* well known that women *are* less likely to hold positions of power.

The Pythagorean theorem *states* that in any right triangle, the square of the length of the hypotenuse *equals* the sum of ...

Referring to implications of findings – PRESENT SIMPLE

Our results *highlight / underline / demonstrate* that people who vote for right-wing parties are more self-centered and less altruistic than those who for left-wing parties.

These findings *show / reveal* that ...

Ongoing trends – PRESENT CONTINUOUS

A study conducted by Credit Suisse shows that inequality *is accelerating*.

An increasing number of studies *are investigating* the role of conspiracy theories in undermining democracy.

Saying what you did during your research – PAST SIMPLE

We analysed xyz. We then organized xyz into categories. These categories were used to calculate ...

Usage, Style, and Grammar: 8.1

Grammar Exercises: 6.1 – 6.3

11.3   Abstracts

Objectives – PRESENT SIMPLE

This paper *aims* to shed light on ... / This paper *sheds* light on

In this work we *investigate* [or *investigated*] the role played by color in decision making.

This paper *outlines* a methodology for establishing the potential for verbosity in a language.

The aim of the project *is* [or *was*] to prove that Google Translate is generally more efficient that a non-native translator.

Announcing the novelty of your work (often used in the first sentence of the abstract) – PRESENT PERFECT

We *have developed* an innovative method to teach English to animals.

Saying what you did during your research – PAST SIMPLE

We *analysed* xyz. We then *organized* xyz into categories. These categories *were used* to calculate ...

The PRESENT PERFECT is NOT used to say what you did in the lab or during your study.

We have analysed xyz. We have then organized xyz into categories. These categories have been used to calculate ...

English for Writing Research Papers: 13

100 Tips to Avoid Mistakes: 1-10

Grammar Exercises: 19

Writing Exercises: 10.1

11.4   Introduction / Discussion

Background info. Situations that started in the past and continue into the present - PRESENT PERFECT

The sea level *has changed* throughout the Earth's history and will continue to do so. [cf The sea level *changes* every year.]

Over the last 60 years English *has transformed* itself from a predominantly writer-oriented language to a reader-oriented language. [cf If language *transforms* our thinking, do specific languages *transform* it in different ways?]

Use the PRESENT PERFECT and NOT the PRESENT SIMPLE:

- with reference to a present situation, you state how long (in days, years, months etc) this situation has been operative.

- when you tell readers that this is the first (second, third, etc) time that something has been done.

They are many years that we *use* this system. // We *use* this system since many years.

It is the first time that we *use* this system.

This is only the second time that such a result *is* published in the literature.

We *have used* this system for many years.

It is the first time that we *have used* this system.

This is only the second time that such a result *has been published* in the literature.

Reviewing the literature: time mentioned or implied – SIMPLE PAST

In 2015 / A decade ago Alvarez *published* her first account of ...

There have been many examples in the literature on parapsychology, the most recent *was* [Shaw 2027].

Recently, Griggs *made* the surprising discovery that ...

11.4   Introduction / Discussion (cont.)

Reviewing the literature: time possibly not important – **PRESENT PERFECT**

Two theories *have been proposed* to answer this question [Hamnet, Greenslade].

Many articles *have been published* on this subject [Littleton 2017, Marks 2020, Johnston 2027].

Use the PRESENT PERFECT in the Review of the Literature when the sense is past to present.

Typically, the PRESENT PERFECT is used to indicate previous works without saying exactly when the work was published; or if specifying dates, to suggest that similar work is being carried out now and will be in the future.

Prefer the PRESENT PERFECT when referring to the literature if both the following conditions apply:

i) what has been found is more important than when it was found, and

ii) there is no accompanying time reference

Use the PAST SIMPLE when a specific date is mentioned or when you mention what you did in your research.

English for Writing Research Papers: 14, 15

100 Tips to Avoid Mistakes: 11-15

Grammar Exercises: 20

Writing Exercises: 10.2-10.5

11.5 Methods

Explaining procedures, experiments - PRESENT SIMPLE

A cloze procedure *is* a technique in which words *are deleted* from a passage according to a word-count formula. The passage *is presented* to students, who *insert* words as they *read* to complete the text.

In our procedure the students *are* first split into groups by level. This grouping *enables* the teacher to ...

The advantages of this procedure *are*: i) a lot of time *can be saved*, ii) students *are placed* into groups automatically ...

Explaining procedures, experiments – PAST SIMPLE (OFTEN IN PASSIVE FORM)

Our team developed the plan for the operation and research program. An IBM PC *was used* for the calculation of ... The samples *were then tested* for ... The results showed that ... [passive form – it is clear who was responsible for the actions, i.e. the authors]

The aim of our procedure *was* to find a way for teachers to place students into groups. We *used* GroupSoft, a dedicated software package (GS Inc, California) which automatically places students into groups. We *adapted* the software by adding an additional step in which students are preliminarily grouped by age. [This and the following examples highlight the use of *we* + active].

In the second experiment, we *assumed* that ... thus we *decided* to eliminate the first two steps. This *meant* that we *placed* the students immediately into ...

Learn more about the passive form (13.4).

English for Writing Research Papers: 17

11.6   Results

Both PRESENT SIMPLE and PAST SIMPLE are possible. Check with similar papers from your chosen journal to see which tense authors typically use.

The results *show* that x = y.

The results *showed* that x=y.

English for Writing Research Papers: 17

100 Tips to Avoid Mistakes: 16-24

Grammar Exercises: 21, 22

Writing Exercises: 10.6, 10.7

11.7 Discussion

The tenses in the Discussion are used in the same way as in the Introduction, Methods and Results.

English for Writing Research Papers: 16

100 Tips to Avoid Mistakes: 25-26

Grammar Exercises: 23.5

Writing Exercises: 10.8, 10.9

11.8 Conclusions

Summarizing what you have done in the paper – PRESENT PERFECT

We *have presented* a new didactic methodology for teaching Chinese. We *have shown* that ... We *have described* three cases where ...

Summarizing what you did in the lab / during your research – PAST SIMPLE

Our tests *showed* that the children in our sample *were* capable of learning complex constructions much more quickly than adults.

Ongoing research or plans for the future – PRESENT SIMPLE AND PRESENT CONTINUOUS

We *plan* (or *are planning*) to conduct further experiments in order to confirm that women are more intelligent than men.

We *are currently investigating* whether politicians are totally motivated by helping themselves. We *aim* to discover whether they only help people similar to them or whether there is also an element of helping others. This will be the topic of a future paper.

English for Writing Research Papers: 19

100 Tips to Avoid Mistakes: 27-29

Grammar Exercises: 24

Writing Exercises: 10.10-10.13

Chapter 12
Punctuation, Genitive

Punctuation is a vast area of language usage. For full details see:

Usage, Style, and Grammar, Chapter 25

Below are just some key points that frequently cause problems in research manuscripts.

A. Wallwork, *Essential English Grammar and Communication Strategies*,
English for Academic Research, https://doi.org/10.1007/978-3-030-95612-7_12

130

12.1   Capitalization of first letters in a word

Academic titles, degrees, subjects (of study), departments, institutes, faculties, universities

Titles of job positions generally have an initial capital letter, particularly in formal documents (e.g. CVs, biographies for conferences) and when the position is held only by one person (in such cases *a/an* is not required). If the position is held by more than one person (*a/an* required), then no initial capitals are not necessary though may still be found

She is now an Associate Professor at Nanjing University of Traditional Chinese Medicine.

Titles of degrees that are followed by the subject of study have an initial capital letter

Subjects (mathematics, anthropology, history) have no initial capitalization when they are being talked about as subjects of study. However, when they are part of the name of a department, institute or faculty, they require initial capitalization

Short resume: Professor Wang has a Bachelor of Arts in medicine, and a Master's in alternative medicine.

department, institute, faculty and *university* (and similar words) only require capitalization when referring to a specific department, university etc.

From 1891 to 1931 he was Professor of Mathematics and Descriptive Geometry at the Technical University of Munich.

The Faculty of Economics at the University of Bangkok has a long history of …

Days, months, countries, nationalities, spoken languages

Days, months, countries, nationalities (including people who are part of the African diaspora) and languages all have an initial capital letter e.g. *Monday, January, Iran, Iranian, Black*

north(ern), south(ern), east(ern) and *west(ern)* only require initial capitalization when these are official regions e.g. *North Korea* and *South Korea* (these are two separate countries), but *northern Italy* and *southern Italy* (these are geographical areas within the same country).

Generally with initial capitalization: *the West, the Middle East, the Far East.*

Figures, tables, sections etc; steps, phases, stages etc

Capitalize the initial letter when you refer to <u>numbered</u> *sections, figures, tables, appendices, schedules, clauses, steps, phases, stages* etc,

12.1 Capitalization of first letters in a word (cont.)

Do not capitalize the initial letter of *section, figure, table, appendix, schedule, clause, stage* etc when there is no number associated.

Not all journals adopt the guidelines above.

See *the section 2* for further details.

See *step 1* above.

See the *Appendix* for further details.

These tasks will be accomplished in *phase 2* of the project.

See *Section 2* for further details.

See *Step 1* above.

See the *appendix* for further details.

These tasks will be accomplished in *Phase 2* of the project.

Titles of papers and headings

Check your journal's style. If initial capital letters are required by your journal for the title of a paper, use them for:

- the first word
- all other words except: *a, the, it, them, an,* all prepositions (*by, from, of* etc)

Do not use a period (.) at the end of a title.

A Guide To The Use Of English In Scientific Documents

A guide to the use of english in scientific documents.

12.1 Capitalization of first letters in a word (cont.)

A Guide to the Use of English in Scientific Documents

A guide to the use of English in scientific documents

Usage, Style, and Grammar: 24

Writing Exercises: 1.7, 1.8

12.2 Apostrophes

Do not use an apostrophe to make acronyms and dates plural.

Remember that contracted forms are not generally used in research manuscripts

We bought six *PC's*.

Our institute was founded in the *2010's*.

Let's now turn to Theorem 2, where *we'll* learn that *it's* essential to ...

The experiment *can't /couldn't* be repeated.

We bought six *PCs*.

Our institute was founded in the *2010s*.

Let us now turn to Theorem 2, where *we will* learn that *it is* essential to ...

The experiment *cannot / could not* be repeated.

See also 12.6 (genitive).

12.3 Commas

Use a comma:

- to separate two dependent clauses. This is often the case with clauses introduced *by, if, when, as soon as, after* etc

- in lists of more than two items, use a comma before *and*. However, semicolons (12.5) may be preferable in long lists to divide up groups of items

- to highlight the logical sequences of a phrase in a sentence

- after sentences that begin with an adverb that is designed to attract the reader's attention (e.g. *clearly, interestingly*) or a link word that indicates you are adding further information or talking about a consequence (e.g. *in addition, consequently*)

- in non-defining relative clauses (8.10)

When the specimen is *dry remove* it from the recipient.

There are three advantages of this: costs are lower, deadlines and other constraints are more easily *met and customers* are generally happier.

If the water *boils the* specimen will be ruined. [It seems that it is the water that boils the specimen].

Surprisingly the results were not in agreement with any of the hypotheses. *Moreover in* many cases they were the exact opposite of what had been expected.

The *Thames which* runs through *London is* England's longest river.

When the specimen is *dry, remove* it from the recipient.

There are three advantages of this: costs are lower, deadlines and other constraints are more easily *met, and* customers are generally happier.

If the water *boils, the* specimen will be ruined.

Surprisingly, the results were not in agreement with any of the hypotheses. *Moreover, in* many cases they were the exact opposite of what had been expected.

The *Thames, which* runs through *London, is* England's longest river.

12.3 Commas (cont.)

Commas should be avoided or limited if the sentence contains:

- twenty words or more. Consider rearranging the sentence or writing two separate sentences

- a series of very short phrases all separated by commas. Consider rearranging the sentence into longer phrases with fewer commas

12.4   Hyphens

To join one or more words together to indicate that although the expression is made up of multiple words it has the meaning of just one concept.

This is a state-of-the-art technology which is used to .. [*state-of-the-art* is like an adjective, it simply means the most recent / advanced].

The vaccine was initially offered to 90-year-old patients. [*90-year-old* is like an adjective that describes the patients]

To avoid time-consuming decisions, we used row-based flashing.

Control of the interaction is user- not application-driven.

When words, such as those in the examples above, are NOT used as adjectives they do NOT require hyphens.

We examine *the state of the art* in soft robotics.

The patients were *90 years old*.

This procedure is very *time consuming*.

12.5   Semicolons

Semicolons are becoming less and less common in English. Their main use is in lists to clarify what elements in the list belong together.

Several countries are participating in the project, in the following groups: Spain, Cuba and Argentina, France, Morocco and Senegal, and the Netherlands and Indonesia.

Substances are transported in living organisms as: i) solutions of soluble nutrients, ii) solids in the form of food particles, iii) gases such as ...

Figure 1. Three types of classroom arrangements: a, traditional, b, circle, c, U-shaped.

Several countries are participating in the project, in the following groups: Spain, Cuba and Argentina; France, Morocco and Senegal; and the Netherlands and Indonesia.

Substances are transported in living organisms as: i) solutions of soluble nutrients; ii) solids in the form of food particles; iii) gases such as ...

Figure 1. Three types of classroom arrangements: a, traditional; b, circle; c, U-shaped.

= Figure 1. Three types of classroom arrangements: a) traditional, b) circle, and c) U-shaped.

Usage, Style, and Grammar: 25

100 Tips to Avoid Mistakes: 69-72

Writing Exercises: commas 1.1, 1.2; semicolons 1.3, hyphens 1.5, 1.6

12.6   Genitive ('s)

General guidelines

The rules are quite arbitrary and change from noun to noun, and discipline to discipline.

However, if you misuse the genitive it will rarely constitute a serious mistake.

To check whether you have used the genitive correctly, use Google's Scholar advanced search.

When you have two nouns, X and Y, and your meaning is *the Y of X*, <u>often</u> you cannot put them in sequence, for example, *X Y* or *X's Y*. Instead write *the Y of X*.

The *time role* is crucial.

The *time's role* is crucial.

This *time's period* is crucial.

The *role of time* is crucial.

This *period of time* is crucial. (This *time* period is crucial **is also possible**)

If in doubt, write *the x of y* instead of *y x* or *y's*:

London's University is located in ....

The University of London ... (**informally:** London University)

12.6   Genitive ('s) (cont.)

names, referees, colleagues, editors, countries, manufacturers

's is placed immediately after the last letter of the author (or name, country, etc). If the name already ends in an *s* you can still put *'s* (however, some people prefer just to put the apostrophe)

Smith's paper, *Jones's* study, *Jones'* study = the paper by Smith, the study by Jones

Italy's economic crisis. = the crisis in Italy.

When a paper has been written jointly, put an *'s* after *et al.*

A paper by Li et al. (2024) shows that ... In fact Li *et al.'s* paper was the first to ...

When using the plural form of colleague and referee, put just put an apostrophe after the plural s. If only one referee is involved, then put **'s**. if you number the referees put the **'s** after the number.

A paper by Li and colleagues (2024) shows that. In fact Li *and colleagues'* paper showed that ..

The *referees'* comments highlighted that = there are at least TWO referees who wrote the report.

The *referee's* comments are very useful = there is only ONE referee involved

Referee 1's comments were ...

According to the *manufacturer instructions* ...

The Biden's paper is an excellent introduction to the topic.

Biden paper is an excellent introduction to the topic.

We have answered *the referee questions*.

I have just received the *editor decision* along with *the committee report*.

Smith's et al. paper.

12.6   Genitive ('s) (cont.)

According to the *manufacturer's* instructions ...

Biden's paper is an excellent introduction to the topic.

We have answered the *referee's* questions = there is just one referee involved

I have just received the *editor's* decision along with the *committee's* report.

Smith et al. *'s* paper.

names of theories, instruments etc

Use a simple Google search and type in the theory, equation procedure, instrument that you want to check. Normally you will find the correct form along with an explanation.

Below are pairs of sentences showing use with and without the genitive.

As predicted by *Newton's* theory of gravity, ... // *The Newton Theory* of Gravity states that ...

The premise of *Darwin's* theory of evolution is that ... // This work was inspired by *the Darwin Theory* of Evolution.

Fourier's analysis of linear inequality systems highlights ... // We used *Fourier analysis* to evaluate the ...

Tukey's post hoc test was used for the statistical analysis. // *A Tukey* post hoc test was used to ...

non-human subjects

Again the rules are not clear. Check with Google.

The *brain role* is crucial.

The *network task* is to converge to a particular output.

An understanding of *malaria effects* on the region inhabitants is vital.

12.6   Genitive ('s) (cont.)

If you are not sure, you can simply avoid using the genitive, as highlighted by the pairs of sentences in blue below.

The *brain's role* is crucial. **//** The *role of the brain* is crucial.

The *network's* task is to converge to a particular output. **//** The *task of the network* is ...

An understanding of *malaria's effects* on the region's inhabitants is vital. **//** An understanding of *the effects of malaria* on the inhabitants of the region is vital.

The *circle's radius*. **//** The *radius of the circle*.

The approximate time of *the plane's arrival* was calculated. **//** The approximate time of *the arrival of the plane* ...

periods of time

The genitive is used when a time period is used adjectivally

I'm taking *three weeks vacation* next month.

I'm taking *three weeks' vacation* next month. = three weeks of vacation

The genitive is not used when time periods are preceded by *a / the*. Note that the first noun in the noun + noun construction is in the singular form. This is because the first noun functions as an adjective to describe the second noun.

He's on a *three weeks'* vacation.

He's on *a three weeks* vacation.

12.6   Genitive ('s) (cont.)

He's on a *3-week* vacation.

He's on a *three-week* vacation.

Usage, Style, and Grammar: 2

Grammar Exercises: 3

Chapter 13
Verbs

13.1 allow, enable, permit, let

These verbs have the same meaning. They require a personal object: e.g. to allow *someone / the user / the author* to do something.

allow is very commonly used in papers

let + infinitive without *to*. NOT used in the passive form. NOT used frequently in papers (except for phrases such as: *Let x be y. Let us now turn to ...*)

enable is often used when talking about software applications, tools, equipment etc; but not when giving permission

permit only for authorizations, not frequently used in papers

This allows / lets / enables / permits *to make* multiple copies.

They allow *using* a dictionary during the exam.

This allows / enables *the user* to make multiple copies.

They allow *candidates to use* a dictionary during the exam.

= Candidates are allowed to use dictionaries.

allow is often redundant:

This *allows us to reduce* the number of samples needed.

= This *reduces* the number of samples needed.

= The number of samples *can be reduced.*

© The Author(s), under exclusive license to Springer Nature   143
Switzerland AG 2022
A. Wallwork, *Essential English Grammar and Communication Strategies*,
English for Academic Research, https://doi.org/10.1007/978-3-030-95612-7_13

13.1   allow, enable, permit, let (cont.)

Usage, Style, and Grammar: 11.1

100 Tips to Avoid Mistakes: 56

Grammar Exercises: 11.4, 11.5

Vocabulary Exercises: 5.3

13.2 be vs have

be - *is / was / will be* etc + past participle – **to be** is used as an auxiliary verb to form the passive

have - *has / have / had* + past participle – **to have** is used as an auxiliary verb to form the active

The plant *is grown* a lot in the Mediterranean = it is cultivated. Passive.

The plant *has grown* a lot = it has increased in size. Active.

Demand *is* decreased.

The lecture *is* begun.

The project *had* terminated by the organizers due to lack of funding.

Demand *has* decreased.

The lecture *has* begun.

The project *was* terminated by the organizers.

The project *had* already terminated when I joined the team.

Usage, Style, and Grammar: 10

Grammar Exercises: 10.1 - 10.3

13.3   *-ing* form vs infinitive

Main use

-ing - focuses on an activity

infinitive - focuses on the objective, or on what you have to do to achieve an objective

Learning English is easy. = The process is easy.

To learn English you need to study hard. = If you want to learn ...

Having a good memory is really useful. = The fact of possessing.

To have a good memory you need to do a specialized course. = In order to acquire ... If you want to acquire ...

Other uses of *-ing* and the infinitive.

-ing immediately after *before, after, by, about, on, for, in, to* etc

-ing after *be worth, entail, risk, avoid, spend time*

infinitive after verbs that a) express a purpose or objective, e.g. *would like, want, plan, promise, decide, hope*; b) tell someone what they can do or what we want them to do: *allow, ask, enable, expect, help, instruct, permit, persuade, tell.*

The following expression is frequently used at the end of an email. It requires *hearing* (not *to hear*).

I look forward *to hear* from you.

I look forward *to hearing* from you.

The same rule applies to *contribute, dedicate, devote* and a few other similar verbs.

Professor Smith *contributed to writing* the paper.

The chapter is *dedicated / devoted to analysing* the disadvantages of ....

13.3   *-ing* form vs infinitive (cont.)

Usage, Style, and Grammar: 11.2, 11.3, 11.6

Grammar Exercises: 11.1, 11.2, 11.3

Note the constructions used after:

1) *recommend, propose, suggest, advise*

The survey also showed that 88% of these graduates would *recommend to study* in Scotland.

The manufacturers *recommend to do* the check in advance.

Tagawaki et al have *suggested to do* this in reverse order.

The survey also showed that 88% of these graduates would *recommend <u>studying</u>* in Scotland.

The manufacturers *recommend / advise <u>doing</u>* the check in advance.

= The manufacturers *recommend / advise <u>that user should do</u>* the check in advance.

Tagawaki et al have *suggested <u>doing</u>* this in reverse order.

= Tagawaki et al have *suggested <u>that this should be done</u>* in reverse order.

2) *prevent, stop*

Does parental disapproval *prevent teenagers to drink* alcohol?

How do we *stop doctors to overprescribe* antibiotics?

13.3   *-ing* form vs infinitive (cont.)

Does parental disapproval *prevent teenagers <u>from</u> drinking* alcohol?

How do we *stop doctors [<u>from</u>] overprescribing* antibiotics?

Usage, Style, and Grammar: Appendix 1

Grammar Exercises: 11.6

Vocabulary Exercises: 5.13, 5.35

The dangers of the *-ing* form (gerund) with no subject

The two sentences below are ambiguous because it is not 100% clear what the subjects of *driving* and *consuming* are.

If you take your young daughter in the car, don't let her put her head out of the window *while driving*. [Who is driving? You or your young daughter?]

After consuming twenty bottles of wine, the professor presented the awards to the fifty best PhD students. [Who drank the wine? The professor or the students?]

If you take your young daughter in the car, don't let her put her head out of the window while *you are driving*.

After the fifty best PhD students had consumed twenty bottles of wine, the professor presented them with the awards.

Below is another ambiguous sentence.

13.3   *-ing* form vs infinitive (cont.)

This will improve performance *keeping* clients satisfied.

Does this mean: A) the way to improve performance is if clients are kept satisfied? or B) as a consequence of improving performance clients will be satisfied?

To show the real meaning, insert *by* to answer question A, or *thus* to answer question B.

This will improve performance *by keeping* clients satisfied. = If clients are satisfied, performance will improve.

This will improve performance *thus keeping* clients satisfied. = If performance improves clients will be satisfied. Alternatively: This will improve performance and clients *will (thus) be satisfied.*

Note the difference between these four sentences.

To download movies you just need to go on this website. = If you want to download ...

Downloading movies takes only a few seconds. = The process of downloading ...

By downloading movies illegally we are contributing to stifling creativity. = If / When we download movies ...

They download movies illegally, *thus depriving* people of their livelihood. = The result is that we deprive ...

Usage, Style, and Grammar: 11.7, 11.8, 11.9

Vocabulary Exercises: 2.15

Writing Exercises: 4.6

13.4 Passive form

The passive is formed like this:

Active: They *built* a new road. (past simple)

Passive: A new road *was built*. (past simple of *to be* + past participle)

Active: They *are building* a new road. (present continuous)

Passive: A new road *is being built*. (present continuous of *to be* + past participle)

The passive is generally used:

* to describe processes. The focus is NOT on who or what carried out the actions. The most important item is the subject of the sentence. Typically the passive is found in the Methods section

* when making general references to the literature or to what is happening in the world in general

* when it is unnecessary, difficult, or impossible to identify the originator of the action

* to report what is commonly believed to be true

In the examples below the passive form is preferable, unless it is essential to state who carried out the action.

The rust *was removed* by acid-treatment.

= We *removed* the rust by acid-treatment.

An aerosol solution *was added* to make the flame front visible.

= We *added* an aerosol solution to make the flame front visible.

Several attempts *have been made* to explain this phenomenon [17, 24, 33].

= Several researchers *have attempted* to explain this phenomenon [17, 24, 33].

Much progress *is being made* in the field of telecommunications.

= The government *are making* much progress in the field of telecommunications.

The surface of the steel piping *was fractured*.

= Something *had caused* the steel piping to fracture.

13.4   Passive form (cont.)

Usage, Style, and Grammar: 10.4

Grammar Exercises: 10

Writing Exercises: 7.16

100 Tips to Avoid Mistakes: 7, 20, 43

Writing Exercises: 7.16

Chapter 14
Word Order

14.1   subject + verb + direct object + indirect object

Normal word order in English: 1) subject, 2) verb, 3) direct object, 4) indirect object. Keep these four parts as close as possible together.

They submitted their paper to the editor.

1. subject (*they*)
2. verb (*submitted*)
3. direct object (*their paper*)
4. indirect object (*the editor*)

In examples 1-4 below the subject is indicated in *italics*. In 5-6 the direct object is underlined.

Were used *several different methods* in the experiments.

In the survey participated *350 subjects*.

Among the factors that influence the choice of parameters are *time and cost*.

With these values are associated *a series of measurements*.

The authors received from the editor the referees' report.

They conducted with a microscope the research.

A. Wallwork, *Essential English Grammar and Communication Strategies*,
English for Academic Research, https://doi.org/10.1007/978-3-030-95612-7_14

14.1 subject + verb + direct object + indirect object (cont.)

Several different methods were used in the experiments.

A total of 350 subjects participated in the survey.

Time and cost are among the factors that influence the choice of parameters.

A series of measurements are associated with these values.

The authors received <u>the referees' report</u> from the editor.

They conducted <u>the research</u> with a microscope.

14.2 Decide which subject is best and put it at the beginning of the sentence

Often there can be more than one possible subject for your sentence.

Einstein loved science.

Science fascinated Einstein.

In the examples below, probably the first is best as it focuses on the novelty of something, but it may depend on what you want your readers to focus on.

Our new feature for the calculation of X will be particularly interesting for researchers in this field.

X can now be calculated with a new feature which will be particularly interesting for researchers in this field.

If you put the subject first in your sentence, it:

- Forces you to think what the best subject is.
- Reader doesn't have to read complete sentence to discover what it is about.
- Forces you to use shorter sentences and be more direct.
- Reduces the number of words needed.
- Reduces the number of mistakes.

Putting the subject first generally leads to shorter sentences. The blue sentence below contains 27 words less than the red sentence.

We have mentioned a number of different factors that can improve one's writing of scientific papers, however there is one factor that is even more important than the others (i.e. conciseness, sentence length, blah blah and blah blah, using verbs instead of nouns) and this factor is rarely taken into consideration by writers although it is absolutely fundamental; that factor is, of course, putting the subject at the beginning of the sentence.

14.2 Decide which subject is best and put it at the beginning of the sentence (cont.)

Putting the subject at the beginning of the sentence is fundamental in improving one's writing of scientific papers. However, unlike the other factors (i.e. conciseness, sentence length, using verbs instead of nouns) it is rarely taken into consideration by writers.

14.3 Don't separate subject and the verb.

The result, after the calculation has been made, can be used to determine Y.

This sampling method, when it is possible, is useful because it allows ....

These steps, owing to the difficulties in measuring the weight, require some simplifications.

After the calculation has been made, the result can be used to determine Y.

When this sampling method is possible, it allows us ...

Owing to the difficulties in measuring the weight, these steps require some simplifications.

= These steps require some simplifications, owing to the difficulties in measuring the weight

14.4 Don't separate the verb from its direct object.

We can *associate with these values* a high cost, higher overheads, a significant increase in man-hours and several other problems.

We can *associate* a high cost, higher overheads, a significant increase in man-hours and several other problems *with these values*.

We can *associate* a high cost *with these values*, *along with* higher overheads, a significant increase in man-hours and several other problems.

We can *associate several factors with these values*: a high cost, higher overheads, a significant increase in man-hours and several other problems.

14.5   Put the main verb near the beginning of the sentence.

Various European languages including Italian, and Portuguese, along with Hindi, Russian and Chinese (which has only recently been added to this list), can be learned using this method.

Various languages can be learned using this method. These include European languages such as Italian and Portuguese, along with Hindi, Russian and Chinese. Chinese has only recently been added to this list.

If you use an ACTIVE form, then the verb will be near the <u>beginning</u> of the sentence instead of the <u>end</u>. This makes the sentence easier to read.

English for Writing Research Papers (2016 edn.): Chapter 2

Usage, Style, and Grammar: 16

100 Tips to Avoid Mistakes: 57-60

Grammar Exercises: 14.1, 14.2

Writing Exercises: 2.1 – 2.11

160

14.6   Adjectives

Place adjectives before the noun they describe, or use an alternative construction.

This is a paper *interesting* for PhD students.

We examined a patient, 30 years old, to investigate whether …

This is an *interesting* paper.

This paper is *interesting* for PhD students.

This is a paper *that is particularly interesting* for PhD students.

We examined a 30-year-old patient to investigate whether …

We examined a patient, who was 30 years old, to investigate whether …

Do not insert an adjective between two nouns or before a noun that it does not describe.

The editor main interface

The algorithm computational complexity

The main document contribution

The main interface of the editor

The computational complexity of the algorithm

The main contribution of the document

14.6 Adjectives (cont.)

Usage, Style, and Grammar: 18.1-18.3

Grammar Exercises: 14.3

14.7 Adverbs: basic rules

The following types of adverbs:

frequency (e.g. *never, often, sometimes, occasionally*)

time (*recently, currently*)

also and *only*

certainty (e.g. *probably, certainly definitely*)

consequence (e.g. *thus, therefore*)

are located:

BEFORE THE <u>MAIN VERB</u>.

Dying neurons do not *usually* <u>exhibit</u> these biochemical changes.

We *thus* <u>decided</u> to implement a new strategy.

These will *probably* not <u>have</u> a major effect.

The old system should *thus / therefore / consequently* not be <u>used</u>.

The new system should be used. It should *also* be <u>integrated</u> with all the old data.

IMMEDIATELY BEFORE THE <u>SECOND AUXILIARY</u> WHEN THERE ARE TWO AUXILIARIES.

Language would *never* <u>have</u> arisen as a set of arbitrary terms if … .

Late complications may not *always* <u>have</u> been noticed.

AFTER THE PRESENT AND PAST TENSES OF 'TO BE'.

The answer given by the machine *is always* correct.

14.8   Adverbs that typically go at the beginning of the sentence

The following types of adverbs are usually located at the beginning of a phrase, but may sometimes appear later.

- add further information (e.g. *in addition, furthermore, further, moreover*)

- attract attention or express some kind of emotion (*surprisingly, intriguingly, regrettably, unfortunately*)

- enumerate points (e.g. *firstly, secondly, finally*)

- indicate a concession or begin an explanation (e.g. *since, although, even though*)

- indicate a time period (e.g. *in the last few years / decades, to date*)

- indicate an alternative (*alternatively*)

- specify (*specifically, in particular*)

For this reason / It follows that / As a consequence / As a result, it is not a good idea to use the old system.

The new system should be used. *In addition*, it should be integrated with all the data from the previous project.

Firstly, the component is subjected to ..

Interestingly, few works have examined …

Some adverbs tend to go in the middle of a sentence and not at the beginning.

This tool costs $400, *whereas* that tool costs $300

Others can appear in more than one position.

On the other hand, China has

China, *on the other hand*, has ...

In fact, Japan is ...

Japan, *in fact*, is ...

14.9   Adverbs of manner

An adverb of manner indicates how something is done. They are generally placed directly after the verb, or after the direct object

The curve rises *steadily / gradually / rapidly / slowly / constantly* until it reaches a peak at 1.5.

Our results agree *well / perfectly* with their findings.

This work was carried out *carefully / accurately / thoroughly.*

Usage, Style, and Grammar: 17

Grammar Exercises: 14.7-14.14

14.10 Past participles

In most cases past participles can always go <u>after</u> the noun, but in many cases they cannot go <u>before</u>. So, put them <u>after</u> and you will probably be right!

In some cases both positions are possible. When the past participle is located after the noun it is often followed by further details.

Be careful with *used*. Before the noun it means 'second hand', after the noun it means 'which is used'.

It shows details of all the *found results*.

We detail the *main involved social actors* along with all the *consumed materials*.

The *considered alternatives* and the way the problem is structured may vary in interpretation.

This was the *used application* by the testers.

It shows details of all the *results found*.

We detail the *main social actors involved* along with all the *materials consumed*.

The *alternatives considered* and the way the problem is structured may vary in interpretation.

This was the *application used* by the testers.

I bought a *used car*. [= a second-hand car]

Usage, Style, and Grammar: 18.4

Grammar Exercises: 14.4

14.11   Mistakes to Avoid

1) Don't insert parenthetical information between subject and verb.

English, although currently the international language of business, may one day be replaced by Spanish or Chinese.

The above construction separates the subject (*English*) from the verb (*may*).

The constructions below keep the subject and verb together.

Although English is currently the international language of business, it may one day be replaced by Spanish or Chinese.

English may one day be replaced by Spanish or Chinese, *even though* it is currently the international language of business.

English is currently the international language of business. *However*, it may one day be replaced by Spanish or Chinese.

2) Don't create strings of nouns

Do not indiscriminately put nouns and adjectives in front of each other.

art state technology

state-of-the-art technology

Check on Google Scholar that your proposed string of nouns already exists and has been used by native English-speaking authors.

If it has NOT been used by native English-speaking authors, then you need to change the order of the words, which normally entails inserting some prepositions.

14.11 Mistakes to Avoid (cont.)

an internal strains collection

for sample initial purification

the WHO main recommendations

environmental performance improvement indicators

a collection of internal strains

for the initial purification of samples

the main recommendations of WHO

indicators of improvements in environmental performance

3) Don't put the negative part of a concept at the end of a sentence, put it near the beginning

Negative information tends to be key information. Don't surprise the reader by putting it at the end. Give the bad news first!

Finding a candidate with all the right qualifications, with a high level of communications skills, a good knowledge of at least two languages and a friendly personality is *not an easy task*.

It is *not easy* to find …

14.11   Mistakes to Avoid (cont.)

4) Don't be ambiguous. Put the elements in a sentence in the most logical order.

They delivered food to the elderly residents living locally in a large box.

Like Sandra, he had dark brown hair, with enormous black eyebrows, a moustache and a short beard.

They delivered food in a large box to the elderly residents living locally.

He had enormous black eyebrows, a moustache and a short beard, and like Sandra he had dark brown hair. //// Like Sandra he had dark brown hair. His eyebrows were black and enormous, and he had a moustache and a short beard

5) Don't delay the subject with an impersonal expression such as *it is advisable, probable, likely, mandatory that*

It is advisable that a foreign language should be learned at a young age.

It is interesting to note that …

It is probable that X will happen.

A foreign language should be learned at a young age.

Note that …

X will *probably* happen.

14.11   Mistakes to Avoid (cont.)

English for Writing Research Papers (2016 edn.): Chapter 2

Usage, Style, and Grammar: 16.10 – 16.12

100 Tips to Avoid Mistakes: 63

How is the Book Organized?

The book is organized into 14 'chapters' on various aspects of English usage. The chapters have self-explanatory titles, with the exception of Chapter 13 (Verbs and Forms) which contains items that would not fit well in the other chapters!

Within each chapter, there are short guidelines and examples of both good and bad English.

The good sentences are written in blue, the bad in red. You may find that this color distinction is not available in the version of the book that you have. Don't worry! The icons below are designed to clearly show what sentences are examples of good and bad English.

 This sentence is NOT in good English.

 This sentence is in good English.

 Warning! Indicates a serious error that is typically made.

 Outlines a useful strategy.

 Reference to books written by Adrian Wallwork in the *English for Academic Research* series.

If there is no smiley, and the sentence is in blue it means the sentence is correct, if it is in red it is incorrect.

Are the guidelines given in this book 100% applicable in all cases?

No. Each scientific discipline (and indeed sub-discipline) tends to use English in very specific ways that are not consistent across disciplines. Also, not all native-speaking authors apply the same rules of grammar and style.

So, if in your chosen journal you find examples of 'rules' that seem to go against the 'rules' in this book, always follow your journal.

© The Author(s), under exclusive license to Springer Nature Switzerland AG 2022
A. Wallwork, *Essential English Grammar and Communication Strategies*, English for Academic Research, https://doi.org/10.1007/978-3-030-95612-7

Other Books in this Series

The first two titles below are the most recent:

Writing an Academic Paper in English: Intermediate Level

Giving an Academic Presentation in English: Intermediate Level

English for Research: Usage, Style, and Grammar – a much more comprehensive version of the book you are reading now.

English for Academic Research: Grammar / Vocabulary / Writing Exercises - these three books of exercises practice the rules and guidelines given in this manual.

English for Writing Research Papers - everything you need to know about how to write a paper that referees will recommend for publication.

100 Tips to Avoid Mistakes in Academic Writing and Presenting – outlines the most serious mistakes you may make when writing and presenting. The book explains the implications of making the mistake, the solution and the positive impact that the solution will have.

How to find further information about the points discussed in this book

The table below shows where you can find further details of the points explained in this book in the books in the English for Academic Research series.

1 = this book

2 English for Academic Research: Grammar, Usage, and Style

3 English for Academic Research: Grammar Exercises

4 English for Academic Research: Writing Exercises

5 English for Academic Research: Vocabulary Exercises

6 English for Academic Research: 100 tips to avoid mistakes in academic writing and presenting

The Author

Adrian Wallwork is from Manchester (UK) but has spent most of his adult life in Italy. He is the author and editor of the English for Academic Research series, along with several course books for OUP and CUP, six books for the BBC, Scholastic and BEP. His latest publications are a series of discussion resource books (https://tefl-discussions.com/).

Adrian has fifteen years of experience teaching academic / scientific English to PhD students with students from over 40 countries. He has held courses and presented at conferences in China, France, Germany, Italy, Poland, Spain, Switzerland and the UK.

Adrian runs **English For Academics (e4ac.com)** a scientific English editing agency with his wife Anna Southern.

A. Wallwork, *Essential English Grammar and Communication Strategies*, English for Academic Research, https://doi.org/10.1007/978-3-030-95612-7

Learn with English for Academics (e4ac.com) and the *English for Academic Research* Series Published by SpringerNature

The author offers several online courses to help students and teachers of academic English. Consult e4ac.com to learn more about the courses plus feedback from students and organizers.

For details contact: adrian.wallwork@gmail.com

© The Author(s), under exclusive license to Springer Nature
Switzerland AG 2022
A. Wallwork, *Essential English Grammar and Communication Strategies*,
English for Academic Research, https://doi.org/10.1007/978-3-030-95612-7

Full Table of Contents

© The Author(s), under exclusive license to Springer Nature
Switzerland AG 2022
A. Wallwork, *Essential English Grammar and Communication Strategies*,
English for Academic Research, https://doi.org/10.1007/978-3-030-95612-7

Index

4.3 = chapter 4, section 3 (i.e. this topic is discussed in a subsection of a chapter) 7 = chapter 7 (i.e. this topic is discussed in an entire chapter)